The WONDER of SMALL THINGS

POEMS OF PEACE & RENEWAL

Edited by
James Crews

Foreword by
Nikita Gill

Storey Publishing

The mission of Storey Publishing is to serve our customers by publishing practical information that encourages personal independence in harmony with the environment.

Edited by Liz Bevilacqua
Art direction and book design by Alethea Morrison
Text production by Jennifer Jepson Smith
Illustrations by © Vicki Turner

Storey books are available at special discounts when purchased in bulk for premiums and sales promotions as well as for fund-raising or educational use. Special editions or book excerpts can also be created to specification. For details, please send an email to special.markets@hbgusa.com.

Storey Publishing
210 MASS MoCA Way
North Adams, MA 01247
storey.com

Storey Publishing, LLC is an imprint of Workman Publishing Co., Inc., a subsidiary of Hachette Book Group, Inc., 1290 Avenue of the Americas, New York, NY 10104

ISBNs: 978-1-63586-644-5 (paperback); 978-1-63586-645-2 (ebook); 978-1-66863-263-5 (downloadable audio)

Printed in the United States by Lakeside Book Company (interior) and PC (cover)
10 9 8 7 6 5 4 3 2 1

Library of Congress Cataloging-in-Publication Data on file

What if wonder was the ground of our gathering?

Ross Gay

———————————

Sometimes, love looks like small things.

Tracy K. Smith

CONTENTS

Foreword, Nikita Gill xi

What Brings Us Alive, James Crews 1

Wendell Berry, The Peace of Wild Things 5

Ted Kooser, In Early April 6

Paula Gordon Lepp, Can You Hear It? 7

Ellen Rowland, What Branches Hold 8

James Crews, Awe 9

Albert Garcia, Ice 10

Andrea Potos, Crocheting in December 11

James Armstrong, First Snow 12

Diana Whitney, Cathedral 13

Joseph Bruchac, Tutuwas 14

Reflective Pause: Let Wonder Guide You 15

Rita Dove, Horse and Tree 16

Michael Kleber-Diggs, The Grove 17

Toi Derricotte, Cherry Blossoms 18

Julia Alvarez, Locust 20

Laure-Anne Bosselaar, Lately, ... 22

Maggie Smith, First Fall 23

Nikita Gill, The Forest 24

Kai Coggin, Essence 25

January Gill O'Neil, For Ella 26

Ross Gay, Sorrow Is Not My Name 27

Reflective Pause: A Time for Everything..28

Mark Nepo, Under the Temple..29

Marjorie Saiser, Crane Migration, Platte River.........................30

Ellen Rowland, The Way the Sky Might Taste.........................32

Lorna Crozier, First Kiss...33

Alison Prine, Long Love...34

James Crews, Here with You..35

Alison Luterman, Heavenly Bodies...36

Jacqueline Jules, The Honeybee...38

Reflective Pause: Choosing Peace 39

AE Hines, What Did You Imagine Would Grow?.....................40

Rachel Michaud, Crossing Over...41

Mark Nepo, Stopped Again by the Sea......................................42

Carolyn Chilton Casas, Ocean Love..43

Angela Narciso Torres, Self-Portrait as Water.........................44

George Bilgere, Swim Lessons...46

Rudy Francisco, Water...47

Rosemerry Wahtola Trommer, Belonging..................................48

Danusha Laméris, Dust...49

Li-Young Lee, To Hold...50

Holly Wren Spaulding, Primitive Objects..................................51

Donna Hilbert, Ribollita...52

Ada Limón, Joint Custody...53

Lucy Griffith, Attention..54

Reflective Pause: The Place of Attention 55

Peg Edera, Harbors of Miracle..56

Natalie Goldberg, Home..58

Rebecca Baggett, Chestnut 59

Zeina Azzam, Hugging the Tree.....................................60

Linda Hogan, Home in the Woods 61

Danusha Laméris, Nothing Wants to Suffer 62

Reflective Pause: The Awe of Aliveness 63

Kimberly Blaeser, The Way We Love Something Small 64

Brooke McNamara, Listen Back 65

Michelle Wiegers, Slow Down 66

Joshua Michael Stewart, November Praise............................68

Susan Varon, The Gentle Dark.......................................69

Jacqueline Suskin, Sunrise, Sunset 70

Joanne Durham, Sunrise Sonnet for My Son............................71

Meghan Dunn, Ode to Butter...72

Robbi Nester, Rot.. 73

Naomi Shihab Nye, Little Farmer 74

James Crews, Tomatoes 76

Sarah Wolfson, What I Like About Beans 77

Susan Musgrave, Tomatoes on the Windowsill
After Rain 78

Mary Jo LoBello Jerome, Tomato Intuition................................79

Leah Naomi Green, Carrot...80

Reflective Pause: Nothing for Granted 81

Jessica Gigot, Amends.. 82

Lahab Assef Al-Jundi, What the Roses Said to Me 83

Rage Hezekiah, Layers... 84

Dorianne Laux, My Mother's Colander.................................. 85

Sue Ann Gleason, Ask Me 86

Paola Bruni, The Lesson.. 88

Meghan Sterling, Chickadee.. 89

Faith Shearin, My Daughter Describes the Tarantula............ 90

Laura Foley, Lost and Found 91

Joy Harjo, Redbird Love 92

Kim Stafford, Wren's Nest in a Shed near Aurora 94

Sharon Corcoran, Encounter 95

José A. Alcántara, Archilochus Colubris............................... 96

Emilie Lygren, Meditation... 97

Margaret Hasse, Art 98

Mark Nepo, Art Lesson 99

Cristina M. R. Norcross, Breathing Peace............................100

Caroline Webster, Expecting 102

Mark Nepo, The Clearing... 103

Laura Foley, What Stillness 104

Reflective Pause: The Gift of Stillness................................ 105

Lisa Zimmerman, Lake at Night 106

Joseph Bruchac, Birdfoot's Grampa 107

Heather Swan, Boy 108

Nikita Gill, Your Soft Heart...109

Joyce Sutphen, From Out the Cave 110

Marilyn McCabe, Web...112

Anne Evans, A New Variant 114

Barbara Crooker, This Summer Day..115

Ted Kooser, A Glint...116

Derek Sheffield, For Those Who Would See 117

Reflective Pause: Winks of Calm 118

Sally Bliumis-Dunn, Aubade 119

Kim Stafford, Advice from a Raindrop.....................................120

Danusha Laméris, Let Rain Be Rain 121

Nina Bagley, Gathering 122

Stuart Kestenbaum, Holding the Light 123

Alberto Ríos, The Broken..124

Alfred K. LaMotte, Gentle 125

Patricia Clark, Creed 126

Michael Simms, Sometimes I Wake Early 127

Marjorie Moorhead, Head in the Clouds..................................128

Joseph Fasano, Letter 129

Penny Harter, Just Grapefruit 130

Jane Kenyon, In Several Colors...131

Kathryn Petruccelli, Instinct...132

Terri Kirby Erickson, Goldfinch 134

Ada Limón, It's the Season I Often Mistake............................ 136

Katherine J. Williams, Late August, Lake Champlain...........137

Laura Ann Reed, Fortitude 138

Nathan Spoon, Poem of Thankfulness...................................... 139

Annie Lighthart, Let This Day 140

Reflective Pause: Let It Change.. 141

Laura Grace Weldon, Common Ground................................. 142

Rena Priest, Tour of a Salmonberry 143

Rosalie Sanara Petrouske, True North 144

Connie Wanek, Talking to Dad 146

Tyler Mortensen-Hayes, After the Heartbreak........................ 147

Ingrid Goff-Maidoff, The Listening Bridge............................... 149

Brad Peacock, A Morning in Thailand 150

Julia Fehrenbacher, The Only Way I Know
    to Love the World.. 151

Jacqueline Suskin, How to Fall in Love with Yourself 152

Brad Aaron Modlin, One Candle Now, Then
    Seven More..153

Judith Chalmer, Pocket 155

Adele Kenny, Survivor...157

Lois Lorimer, Rescue Dog..158

Yvonne Zipter, Seeds 159

David Mook, Milkweed..160

Bradford Tice, Milkweed 161

Jane Hirshfield, Solstice 162

Julie Cadwallader Staub, Reverence 163

Jennifer G. Lai, In My Mind's Coral,
    Mother Still Calls Us from Inside 164

Reflective Pause: Worlds of Wonder 165

Rosemerry Wahtola Trommer, Latent 166

Charles Rossiter, Transformation 167

Tony Hoagland, Field Guide 168

Rage Hezekiah, Lake Sunapee 169

January Gill O'Neil, How to Love 172

Reading Group Questions and Topics for Discussion 173

Poet Biographies 178

Credits 207

Acknowledgments 212

FOREWORD

My grandmother once told me that where there is wonder, there also lives poetry. She told me this on a golden spring day at her home in the countryside while we finally picked the ruby-red strawberries she had planted months ago. She held one up to the dazzling Indian sun and said, "To a poet, even a little strawberry like this is a poem." Something about that moment burns so brightly in my mind, I see it in vibrant Technicolor even though I couldn't have been more than six years old when it happened.

This treasured memory is what I think of when I read this gorgeous anthology. What my grandmother gave to me that day was a sense of wonder that the world around us holds magic in what might be considered small and ordinary. The bird that sings outside your window every morning, or as Maggie Smith says in her gorgeous poem "First Fall," "the leaves rusting and crisping at the edges." All you need to do is see it through the enchanted lens that turns the everyday into the extraordinary. This is precisely what poets do so well. Consider these words by Kai Coggin: "did you know these tiny sprouts these little leaves and baby greens already hold the heavy flavors of their final selves?" This revelation tells us that there is so much we do not know about nature, about what we plant in our own gardens, about the trees and the rivers and towns that surround us.

In the introduction to this anthology, James Crews powerfully reminds us about our natural sense of curiosity, of the quiet adventure that is found even on a peaceful walk. Every poem in this collection is filled with such awe and reminds us of the duty of the poet: to collect that awe and write it down. I consider each of these poems to be a lighthouse that beckons others toward its light, giving them hope and safety. Here, Ross Gay reminds us of how little pieces of wonder become a lifeline, a reason to say, "But look; my niece is running through a field calling my name. My neighbor sings like an angel and at the end of my block is a basketball court."

Mary Oliver once said that it is the job of a poet to stand still and learn to be astonished by the world. If there were ever an anthology that proves her thesis, it would be this one. I hope you read this book and delight in these poems as I have. Read them on a sunny day in the garden or in the safety of your bedroom as the rain falls heavily from the sky. Read them when your heart is heavy and your mind feels fraught. Find in these pages your little moments of peace, nourishment for your soul.

As my grandmother said, where there is wonder, there are poets. And where there are poets, there are also the words you never knew you needed, exactly when you need them most.

Nikita Gill

WHAT BRINGS US ALIVE

My husband, Brad, and I were walking the forest trail near our house one autumn afternoon. I found myself feeling bored and more than a little annoyed, however, with the monotony of our usual walk—the same trees starting to shed their leaves, the same rocky path, and same patches of sunlight breaking through the thinned-out canopy. Then Brad gasped and fell to his knees. I thought something was wrong at first, but no—he had spotted a neon-orange caterpillar inching across the crisp leaves that lined the trail, making its slow way across to the other side. "Have you ever seen anything like this?" Brad asked. I told him I had not. He then pulled out his phone and began to film its movements from every angle while I crouched beside him, not only amazed by this creature but also in awe of Brad's awe for the world around us. In just a moment, our so-called boring walk had transformed into one I would never forget, and I was learning once again how to be more present to the every-day wonders that so often occur right at my feet, right in my own backyard. I thought of all the times I had heard Brad give an audible gasp when he saw the white head of a bald eagle coasting above the Battenkill River, or a baby painted turtle swimming in a stream in the abandoned gravel quarry down the road. "I've never seen this before," Brad said as we stared down at that tiny turtle, the reverence evident in his voice.

That same deep love for the world is present in every one of the poems gathered in this book. Wonder calls us back to the curiosity we are each born with, and it makes us want to move closer to what sparks our attention. Wonder opens our senses and helps us stay in touch with a humbling sense of our own human smallness in the face of unexpected beauty and the delicious mysteries of life on this planet. No matter how we name these sensations, we have all felt some version of awe as we were lifted out of the thinking mind, even if for an instant, and brought more fully back into our bodies. In this way, like mindfulness, wonder and awe root us in the moment, and when we create the space in our lives to feel them, the inevitable result is a deep sense of rest, renewal, and peace. The poet and philosopher Mark Nepo has written: "Wonder is the rush of life saturating us with its aliveness, the way sudden rain makes us smile, the way sudden wind opens our face. And while wonder can surprise us, our daily work is to cultivate wonder in ourselves and in each other." In other words, we don't need to wait for amazement to find us, and we don't have to search for it outside of ourselves either. Like the qualities of kindness and gratitude, which have been the subjects of my previous poetry anthologies, wonder and peace can be cultivated and practiced daily with the people, places, and things we encounter.

Poetry often originates in potent bursts of insight, so it is the perfect medium for deepening our practice of reverence for the world. As you'll see, these poems often shun the sublime in favor of the more ordinary blessings we find immediately at hand. In "It's the Season I Often Mistake," for example, the US Poet Laureate Ada Limón describes mistaking birds for leaves and leaves for birds in early winter: "The tawny yellow mulberry leaves are always goldfinches tumbling across the lawn like extreme elation." You'll find many more moments like this throughout the collection, focusing on wonders and insights so slight, we might be inclined to ignore them. Yet these small joys are what most of us can access, and they are the riches of an attentive, mindful life. In order to hold on to such moments, I have also included reflective pauses throughout the book. These sections welcome you to slow down, reflect on a particular poem, and then practice doing some writing of your own, if you wish. I recommend keeping a journal or notebook nearby as you read each poem, since any piece of good writing can transport you more deeply into your own experience.

You'll come across many poems that find the ready-made awe always available in the natural world. It's become clear to us that our planet is in peril, and while we must work to preserve the beauties of this world, we must also remind ourselves, and the generations to come, of all the small wonders they are fighting to save. As the Nebraska poet Marjorie Saiser writes in "Crane Migration, Platte River," "I am in danger of forgetting the cranes . . . how they came as if from the past, how they came of one mind." We sometimes risk forgetting the wonders held in ourselves and in each other, too. In "Talking to Dad," Connie Wanek confesses that she can still speak with her late father no matter where she is: "I need only the faintest signal like a single thread of what used to be his tennis shirt. Like an empty chair at our table into which a grandchild climbs." In her luminous poem "Nothing Wants to Suffer," Danusha Laméris calls us back to radical empathy with each other, animals, and even objects we often consider inanimate, which also deserve our kindness and wonder. "The chair mourns an angry sitter. The lamp, a scalded moth," she writes. "A table, the weight of years of argument. We know this, though we forget."

These poems call us back to our original creative selves, who were never ashamed to give time and attention to something as simple as moss clinging to a fallen log, or a perfect carrot grown in the garden. As Nikita Gill tenderly reminds us, we always have the capacity to practice peace: "You are still the child who gently places fallen baby birds back in their nests." We might rightly feel harmed by the difficult parts of our lives, and alarmed at the state of our world, the endless appetite of the powerful for war and destruction. But to dwell in the brokenness and worry of our lives would be a disservice to ourselves and future generations, who need permission to cultivate wonder, awe, and delight in the middle of a life that's busy, frightening, and amazing all at the same time. As poets and lovers of poetry, we can share the wonders gathered here far and wide. We can use these poems, reflective pauses, and discussion questions to remember what brings us alive, what helps us all find our own moments worthy of savoring.

James Crews

Wendell Berry

THE PEACE OF WILD THINGS

When despair for the world grows in me
and I wake in the night at the least sound
in fear of what my life and my children's lives may be,
I go and lie down where the wood drake
rests in his beauty on the water, and the great heron feeds.
I come into the peace of wild things
who do not tax their lives with forethought
of grief. I come into the presence of still water.
And I feel above me the day-blind stars
waiting with their light. For a time
I rest in the grace of the world, and am free.

Ted Kooser

IN EARLY APRIL

A tree in blossom is a passing cloud
that floats from some warmer place
then slows and snows itself away,
a blizzard of petals that will take
your breath away if you are there,
aware of what's about you, petals
in drifts on the sidewalk, each
with a delicate fragrance that sticks
to the toe of your shoe as you scuff
your way along. All this can occur
in the space of a day, even an hour.
Can you be present when it happens
or will your thoughts have skipped off
into summer and the life beyond?

Paula Gordon Lepp

CAN YOU HEAR IT?

There are days when,
although I try to open myself
to wonder, wonder just
won't be found. Or perhaps,
it is more accurate to say
on those days I am simply
blind to what the world
has to offer

until I look down, and there,
beside the sidewalk,
are blades of grass completely
enrobed in ice, shimmering
in the glow of the setting sun,
and as they sway and move
into each other, if I listen,
really listen,
even they are singing
faint little bell-notes of joy.

Ellen Rowland

WHAT BRANCHES HOLD

This is the hush you've been seeking
isn't it? Silence lush with listening.
Yes, it's cold, so cold and so?
Haven't you come dressed just for this?
And so you pull the soft wool closer, push
the fleeced collar higher, part
the snow-laden branches
and step in, knowing full well
you will be baptized. Allow yourself
to be called deeper and deeper
into this dense huddle
of gentle bark and quiet drape. Did you
ever think you could be so lost and so found
in the same visible breath?

James Crews

AWE

It's a shiver that climbs the trellis
of the spine, each tingle a bright white
morning glory breaking into blossom
beneath the skin. It can happen anywhere,
anytime, even finding this sleeve of ice
worn by a branch all morning, now fallen
on a bed of snow. You can choose to pause,
pick it up, hold the cold thing in your hand
or not. Few tell us that wonder and awe
are decisions we make daily, hourly,
minute by minute in the tiny offices
of the heart—tilting the head to look up
at every tree turned into a chandelier
by light striking ice in just the right way.

Albert Garcia

ICE

In this California valley, ice on a puddle
is a novelty for children
who stand awkward in their jackets
waiting for the school bus.
They lift off thin slabs
to hold up in the early light
like pieces of stained glass.
They run around,
throw them at each other,
lick them, laughing as their pink tongues stick
to the cold, their breath fogging
the morning gray.
      Between the Sierras
in the distance and a faint film
of clouds, the sun rises
red like the gills of a salmon.
From your porch, watching the kids,
you love this morning more
than any you remember. You hear
the bus rumbling down the road
like the future, hear the squealing
voices, feel your own blood warm
in your body as the kids sing
like winter herons, Ice, ice, ice.

Andrea Potos

CROCHETING IN DECEMBER

We live to learn new ways to hold
summer sun through winter cold.
—*Robert Francis*

I'm wandering the craft store aisles—
yarn bins to the ceiling of blackberry dusk,
lime sherbet, heather bloom,
grape gala and so much more.
I pass them all to find
what will carry me through
the cruel months to come: the softest acrylic
sunny day—a slight sheen on its surface
as if dusted with air of high June.

I fill my arms with skeins.
I will take them home, use what I need
for the warmth of winter gold.

James Armstrong

FIRST SNOW

As you lie in bed,
you can tell it has snowed
by the radiance in the window—
light comes from the ground and not the sky
as if you suddenly lived on the moon.
In that moment, you are back to childhood
when any change of the exterior world
is a change of heart, when the light
tells you what to feel, when you need the sky
and its endless changes.
When that first snow fell,
each snowflake whispered
a secret so intimate
it took the rest of your life to un-believe.
Here it is again.
Your chance to repent.

Diana Whitney

CATHEDRAL

Aquarian sun blazes off the snowpack
blinding me with birdsong,
blue skies and change.

Every year I make a pact
with darkness.

I surrender to the season,
bed down with animals,
eat red meat and chocolate

clad in layers of wool.
But here it is again—sunlight

on my face in the windless
meadow. Actual heat,

not the polar queen's bitter gaze.
A flock of wild turkeys
scores its three-pronged tracks

like runes for me to trace
into the forest. I didn't know
I was waiting for a sign.

In the cathedral of pines
a rough arch, a gold shadow,
the red walls of my heart

expanding in snow.

Joseph Bruchac

TUTUWAS

I know the names
on this land
have been changed,
printed on maps
made by those
who claim their ownership.

Some say nothing survives.

But the wind
still sings
the same song
of our breath.

The hilltop trees
still bend like dancers
in ceremonies
that never ended.

And the little pines,
tutuwas, tutuwas,
lift up, protected
from the weight of snow
by the held-out arms
of their elders.

Let Wonder Guide You

"Tutuwas" finds delight in the simple winter scene of little pines, or tutuwas, as they were once called by Indigenous people of eastern North America, covered in snow. Joseph Bruchac explains that, "'Tutuwas' is the name of a song that is also called 'Little Pines,' which can be heard in various Wabanaki nations throughout New England from Vermont to the Canadian Maritimes, Western Abenaki, Penobscot, Passamaquoddy, Malecite, and Miq'mac. It's usually sung by children and danced by their mothers. The words ask the dancers to move toward each of the four directions, and spin around. The title 'Tutuwas' refers to human babies as well as the small pine trees that are protected by the outstretched arms of their elders." By using a word that applies to the young of both humans and trees, Bruchac reminds us that we are elements of the natural world. We can feel protected by the "held-out arms" of elders who were rooted here.

Invitation for Writing and Reflection

Focus on some plant or animal that draws your attention and describe it in specific detail. Let it speak to your creative, intuitive self, allowing curiosity and wonder to guide you in your exploration.

Rita Dove

HORSE AND TREE

Everybody who's anybody longs to be a tree—
or ride one, hair blown to froth.
That's why horses were invented, and saddles
tooled with singular stars.

This is why we braid their harsh manes
as if they were children, why children
might fear a carousel at first for the way
it insists that life is round. No,

we reply, there is music and then it stops;
the beautiful is always rising and falling.
We call and the children sing back *one more time.*
In the tree the luminous sap ascends.

Michael Kleber-Diggs

THE GROVE

Planted here as we are, see how we want
to bow and sway with the motion of earth
in sky. Feel how desire vibrates within us
as our branches fan out, promise entanglements,
rarely touch. Here, our sweet rustlings. If only
we could know how twisted up our roots
are, we might make vast shelter together—cooler
places, verdant spaces, more sustaining air.
But we are strange trees, reluctant in this
forest—we oak and ash, we pine—
the same the same, not different. All of us
reach toward star and cloud, all of us want
our share of light, just enough rainfall.

Toi Derricotte

CHERRY BLOSSOMS

I went down to
mingle my breath
with the breath
of the cherry blossoms.

There were photographers:
Mothers arranging their
children against
gnarled old trees;
a couple, hugging,
asks a passerby
to snap them
like that,
so that their love
will always be caught
between two friendships:
ours & the friendship
of the cherry trees.

Oh Cherry,
why can't my poems
be as beautiful?

A young woman in a fur-trimmed
coat sets a card table
with linens, candles,
a picnic basket & wine.
A father tips
a boy's wheelchair back
so he can gaze
up at a branched
heaven.
                    All around us
the blossoms
flurry down
whispering,

    Be patient
you have an ancient beauty.

        Be patient,
        you have an ancient beauty.

Julia Alvarez

LOCUST

Weybridge 1998

Happiness surprised me in middle age:
just in the nick of forty I found love,
a steady job, a publisher, a home,
ten acres and a sky-reflecting pond—
a better ending than I'd expected.
We built our own house on a bare hillside
and started planting trees: elm, maples, oak.
Under my second-story writing room
(which was all windows on the southeast side)
we put in locusts for their "instant shade."

By our third anniversary those trees
were grown so tall, it was like climbing up
into a tree house when I went to work,
pulling the mind's ladder up behind me
from the absorbing life I was living.
I tried to focus but those branches filled
with songbirds busy at their nest building,
squirrels scampering to the very edges
of blossoming branches buzzing with bees.
How could I write with all this activity?

It took some getting used to but, of course,
life feeds life. Where'd I get the idea
that art and happiness could never jive?
I felt stupid, wasting so many years.
But I took solace from those locust trees,
known for their crooked, seemingly aimless growth.
We have to live our natures out, the seed
we call our soul unfolds over the course
of a lifetime and there's no going back
on who we are—that much I've learned from trees.

Laure-Anne Bosselaar

LATELY,

      when a branch pulls at my sleeve
like a child's tug, or the fog, reticent & thick,
lifts — & strands of it hang like spun sugar
in branches & twigs, or when a phoebe
trills from the hackberry,
                     I believe such luck
is meant for me. Does this happen to you?
Do you believe at times that a moment
chooses you to remember it & tell about it—
so that it may live again?

Maggie Smith

FIRST FALL

I'm your guide here. In the evening-dark
morning streets, I point and name.
Look, the sycamores, their mottled,
paint-by-number bark. Look, the leaves
rusting and crisping at the edges.
I walk through Schiller Park with you
on my chest. Stars smolder well
into daylight. Look, the pond, the ducks,
the dogs paddling after their prized sticks.
Fall is when the only things you know
because I've named them
begin to end. Soon I'll have another
season to offer you: frost soft
on the window and a porthole
sighed there, ice sleeving the bare
gray branches. The first time you see
something die, you won't know it might
come back. I'm desperate for you
to love the world because I brought you here.

Nikita Gill

THE FOREST

One day, when you wake up,
you will find that you've become a forest.

You've grown roots and found strength in them
that no one thought you had.

You have become stronger
and full of life-giving qualities.

You have learned to take all the negativity around you
and turn it into oxygen for easy breathing.

A host of wild creatures live inside you
and you call them stories.

A variety of beautiful birds nest inside your mind
and you call them memories.

You have become an incredible
self-sustaining thing of epic proportions.

And you should be so proud of yourself,
of how far you have come from the seeds of who you used to be.

Kai Coggin

ESSENCE

I thinned the seeds already sprouting
in the bamboo garden
the radish beet carrot and bean

pulled each birth
out of the earth
and laid it on my tongue
crushed it with my teeth

and did you know these tiny sprouts
these little leaves and baby greens
already hold the heavy flavors of their final selves?

if only we tasted our own essence from birth
knew the transformations to come
were all part of the becoming—

that we had the imprint all along.

January Gill O'Neil

FOR ELLA

I love a wild daffodil,
the one that grows
where she's planted—
along a wooded highway
left to her own abandon,
but not abandoned.
Her big yellow head
leaning toward or away
from the sun. Not excluded
but exclusive, her trumpet
heralds no one, not even
the Canada geese—
their long-necked honks
announcing their journey.
She'll be here less
than a season, grace us
with green slender stems,
strong enough to withstand
rain and spring's early chill.
And when she goes,
what remains she'll bury
deep inside the bulb of her,
take a part of me with her
until she returns.

Ross Gay

SORROW IS NOT MY NAME

after Gwendolyn Brooks

No matter the pull toward brink. No
matter the florid, deep sleep awaits.
There is a time for everything. Look,
just this morning a vulture
nodded his red, grizzled head at me,
and I looked at him, admiring
the sickle of his beak.
Then the wind kicked up, and,
after arranging that good suit of feathers
he up and took off.
Just like that. And to boot,
there are, on this planet alone, something like two
million naturally occurring sweet things,
some with names so generous as to kick
the steel from my knees: agave, persimmon,
stick ball, the purple okra I bought for two bucks
at the market. Think of that. The long night,
the skeleton in the mirror, the man behind me
on the bus taking notes, yeah, yeah.
But look; my niece is running through a field
calling my name. My neighbor sings like an angel
and at the end of my block is a basketball court.
I remember. My color's green. I'm spring.

A Time for Everything

Despite our fears and uncertainties, Ross Gay calls us back to wonder again and again in his poem "Sorrow Is Not My Name." Even the sight of a vulture who "nodded his red, grizzled head at me" can become a source of sudden awe, if we pause long enough to notice the miracle of that creature wearing his "good suit of feathers" then flying off again into the wind. And those "two million naturally occurring sweet things" might make us rapturous as we sing out loud their names: "agave, persimmon, stick ball, the purple okra." In the end, Gay reminds us that the simplest things keep us attached to this difficult yet still praiseworthy world. Our relationships, our home-place, our passions, and the fact that we can still recall them if we wish, give us the resilience to remain "green," to remember that our nature is to keep growing despite the obstacles, and even sometimes because of them.

Invitation for Writing and Reflection

Begin your writing by using the same words that begin Ross Gay's poem, "No matter . . . ," and articulate some of the fearful things that might keep you from delight. See where that repetition leads you, and let your intuition take over as you write from a place of reverence for the simplest things you witness.

Mark Nepo

UNDER THE TEMPLE

The temple hanging over the water is
anchored on pillars that nameless workers
placed in the mud long ago. So never forget
that the mud and the hands of those workers
are part of the temple, too. What frames the
sacred is just as sacred. The dirt that packs
the plant is the beginning of beauty. And
those who haul the piano on stage are the
beginning of music. And those who are
stuck, though they dream of soaring,
are the ancestors of our wings.

Marjorie Saiser

CRANE MIGRATION, PLATTE RIVER

I am in danger of forgetting the cranes,
their black wavering lines in the sky,
how they came as if from the past,
how they came of one mind,
wheeling, swirling over the river.
I am in danger of losing
the purling sound they make,
and the motion of their long wings.
We had stopped the car on the river road
and got out, you and I,
the wind intermittent in our faces
as if it too came from a distant place
and wavered and began again, gusting.
Line after line of cranes
came out of the horizon,
sliding overhead.
The voices of cranes
harsh and exciting.
Something old in me answered.
What did it say? Maybe it said *Kneel.*

I almost forgot the ancient sound,
back in time, back, and back.
The road, the two of us at the guardrail,
low scraggle of weeds flattening and rising
in wind. This is what I must retain:
my knees hit the damp sand of the roadside.
This is what I remember:
you knelt too. We were wordless together
before the birds as they landed on the sandbars
and night came on.

Ellen Rowland

THE WAY THE SKY MIGHT TASTE

The bite of a softened cardamom pod
in a spoonful of Tikka Masala.
Tang of copper, caperberry
other berries, too:
a rasp, a blue, a lingon, elder
lit with lemon, thin slice of moon.
The breath of a first kiss
sweet and deeply surprising.
Dirt on the youngest tongue, the red
flesh of a torn fig eaten
straight from the tree,
the constellation of wings
as champagne leaves the flute.

Lorna Crozier

FIRST KISS

It was like the farm
when it went
electric, remember?

Just like that
you flicked a switch
and it was Genesis.

We saw each other
in our nakedness
though we weren't,

not yet.

Alison Prine

LONG LOVE

blur of years stirs in the room
on a bright February morning

I have studied your face
for ten thousand days

long shadows across the untouched snow
your winter-split fingertips against my spine

tone color of your voice
that has said my name more than any other

ragged with grief, hoarse with desire
warm tenor of dailiness

when our love was illegal
and we were young we promised

not to promise, didn't we
didn't we say we would just begin again

James Crews

HERE WITH YOU

It's too hot on this August afternoon
to move from our places on the couch,
even to slice the peach still waiting
on the counter for the kiss of the knife.

A different kind of hunger keeps me
here with you, rubbing the fine hairs
on your arms that have turned blond
after all those hours in the sun,

and which are just now catching
the light, spinning it into gold I want
to touch over and over, never once
having dreamed I'd ever be this rich.

Alison Luterman

HEAVENLY BODIES

We're falling asleep holding hands.
I can feel his knuckles
rough and dry around the edges.
Hands that work a lathe
five days a week,
cutting, scraping, scouring
the sharp metal.
I've watched them pick their way
up the guitar's neck,
wander over piano keys,
or rub the cat's cheek—
and now, even in sleep
his fingers keep pulsing my palm,
squeezing and releasing
to an inaudible beat.
My own small hand, always cold,
beaches like a starfish
on the reef of his metacarpus.
Twelve years loving and fighting.
How ridiculous
we end up like this—two mis-
matched puzzle pieces,
sanded down to fit.

Clasped and constellated.
There should be
a better name for such
persistence: Stargrit.
Heartlocked. Vowstrung.
Look, love, how we've become
ancient, eternal even,
in our heavenly bodies, wheeling
through the universe without leaving
our bed. Handwoven. Holding on.

Jacqueline Jules

THE HONEYBEE

I almost reacted. Almost
questioned how he could dare
complain about more pots to wash
when I cooked all afternoon.

Then I remembered the honeybee,
how it dies a gruesome death
when its stinger embeds
in human skin. The bee tears
a hole in its belly pulling out
the sac of venom.

A honeybee values peace.
It only stings when threatened,
not over something as petty
as who cooked and who cleaned up.

And certainly not when it could rest,
like I am right now, with feet up
on the couch, while my honey
loads the dishwasher
and scrubs every pot.

Choosing Peace

Life presents us with so many moments when we can decide to react or not. Do we choose peace, or move into negativity? In "The Honeybee," the speaker narrowly avoids a fight with her husband over his idle complaint about having to wash so many pots after she cooked all afternoon. How many times has each of us felt threatened like this, angered by some small, offhand comment a loved one made, perhaps not intending to harm us? Yet, to bring herself back from the brink, she remembers the honeybee, "how it dies a gruesome death when its stinger embeds in human skin." As the speaker points out, "A honeybee values peace" above all things because it can literally mean life and death for that tiny creature. We forget that true peace begins at home, in our individual lives, and even if we can't prevent the larger wars and battles for justice that must rage in the outside world, we can do everything in our power to take care of our own corner of the planet, refusing to engage in a fight over such slight things. Our kind and careful intentions ripple out into the larger world whenever we do what we can to keep the peace we know can be so easily shattered between us.

Invitation for Writing and Reflection

Reflect on a moment when you could have chosen to react with anger, but instead decided to practice peace. How did it feel to exist in that sliver of an instant, choosing peace instead of violence? You might begin, as Jacqueline Jules does here, by saying what you "almost" did.

WHAT DID YOU IMAGINE WOULD GROW?

Before you, I never grew anything.
Never looked at the unbroken ground
and imagined what might sprout there,
that I could coax my own sustenance
from the earth.

I never dislodged the pebbles or dry clay,
and the miracle of food appeared on my table
from the downtown Safeway. The flowers,
orchids, all made of silk.

Before you, there was no garden.
No cherry tomatoes, no peonies or roses,
no sweet-smelling melons swelling
on the ground. You had your tricks
for getting the most from the soil,
the way a saint pulls the best
from a soul.

Before you, my dear, no one bothered.
No one had the patience. No one
stood staring at the thin rocky soil
of me, never walked up and down
my barren rows, rubbing dirt
between his fingers, asking himself:
What shall I plant here?
What precisely will grow?

Rachel Michaud

CROSSING OVER

Did I tell you your eyes are mirrors?
I see who I could be.
Did I tell you your eyes are windows?
A world where I could go.

What is it about your smile?
What is it about your laughter?
What is it about you
that shatters me?

You hold me like a newborn,
tell a bedtime story.
When we rock, when we rock,
who is the boat and who is the sea?

Mark Nepo

STOPPED AGAIN BY THE SEA

My early memories are of
motoring out to sea where we
would cut the engine and hoist
the sails. Then, we'd wait for this
unseen force that some called wind
to carry us away from the streets.
Once in the open sea, it was hard
to think, hard to stay with any one
fear. We always left home to drift
near a deeper home. I guess I've
done this my whole life. For what
is poetry but the drift in search of
a deeper home? What is love but
the hoisting of all we hide until
it carries us away from all that is
hidden? What is peace but the
hammock of a wave that
no one can name?

Carolyn Chilton Casas

OCEAN LOVE

Let me not forget to notice
all the seasons of the ocean
with an awe-filled soul—
equally winter's pounding surf
and summer's gentle swells.
Every bay a changing alchemy
of colors—smoke, sapphire,
aqua, slate, and sky.
Let me not forget to search
September's waters
for the curved backs of whales,
their tails breaching toward the sun,
dorsal fins of dolphins undulating
smoothly in and out of waves
just beyond the breaks.
The ocean's briny smell
fills my lungs with longing
for a simpler life.
She urges me to set my cares aside,
float at peace in her salty arms.

Angela Narciso Torres

SELF-PORTRAIT AS WATER

why does the body feel
  most beautiful underwater—
is what goes through me

  when I break the blue
surface, levels rising as I plumb
  the tub's white womb

this second skin thinner,
  slicker, gleaming wet
as a lacquered bowl

  because the simplest
of molecules—two H's
  one O—love

to love each other, cling
  to what they touch
how this universal solvent

  swallows every hill
fills the hollows
  of my surrender

most forgiving of
  substances, I resolve
to live like you—to fill

and be filled,
to take the shape
of my vessel

dispensing heat
displacing matter
lighter than air

SWIM LESSONS

The pretty lifeguard holds our son to her breast,
counts to three, then plunges him under water
for a full, astonishing second before
lifting him, shocked and sputtering, back
to the sunny morning at the public pool,
and the laughter of his mother and father,
who have betrayed him, who have handed the center
of the universe to a sunburned teenager.

Once again she pulls him to her bosom
and once again the bright young summer,
with its snow cones and beach towels and Coppertone,
closes over his head with a rush, once more
he's far from us, in the drowning element,
until once more a woman brings him gasping
and amazed to the dazzling world,
our little boy, laughing in her arms, beautiful
strangers already laying claim to him.

Rudy Francisco

WATER

When I was six years old,
my brother and my cousins
tried to teach me how to swim.

They did this by throwing me into a pool.
Immediately, my arms became two skinny
brown flailing distress signals.

I think I heard my brother say,
"If he dies, I'm going to be in so much trouble."
I remember them pulling me from the jaws
of the liquid beast before it could devour me whole.
That was the day I almost lost my life.

To anyone brave enough to love me,

Do you know the human body is approximately
sixty percent water? When I walk into a room
full of people, all I see is an ocean.

Rosemerry Wahtola Trommer

BELONGING

And if it's true we are alone,
we are alone together,
the way blades of grass
are alone, but exist as a field.
Sometimes I feel it,
the green fuse that ignites us,
the wild thrum that unites us,
an inner hum that reminds us
of our shared humanity.
Just as thirty-five trillion
red blood cells join in one body
to become one blood.
Just as one hundred thirty-six thousand
notes make up one symphony.
Alone as we are, our small voices
weave into the one big conversation.
Our actions are essential
to the one infinite story of what it is
to be alive. When we feel alone,
we belong to the grand communion
of those who sometimes feel alone—
we are the dust, the dust that hopes,
a rising of dust, a thrill of dust,
the dust that dances in the light
with all other dust, the dust
that makes the world.

Danusha Laméris

DUST

It covers everything, fine powder,
the earth's gold breath falling softly
on the dark wood dresser, blue ceramic bowls,
picture frames on the wall. It wafts up
from canyons, carried on the wind,
on the wings of birds, in the rough fur of animals
as they rise from the ground. Sometimes it's copper,
sometimes dark as ink. In great storms,
it even crosses the sea. Once,
when my grandmother was a girl,
a strong gale lifted red dust from Africa
and took it thousands of miles away
to the Caribbean where people swept it
from their doorsteps, kept it in small jars,
reminder of that other home.
Gandhi said, "The seeker after truth
should be humbler than the dust."
Wherever we go, it follows.
I take a damp cloth, swipe the windowsills,
the lamp's taut shade, run a finger
over the dining room table.
And still, it returns, settling in the gaps
between floorboards, gilding the edges
of unread books. What could be more loyal,
more lonely, and unsung?

Li-Young Lee

TO HOLD

So we're dust. In the meantime, my wife and I
make the bed. Holding opposite edges of the sheet,
we raise it, billowing, then pull it tight,
measuring by eye as it falls into alignment
between us. We tug, fold, tuck. And if I'm lucky,
she'll remember a recent dream and tell me.

One day we'll lie down and not get up.
One day, all we guard will be surrendered.

Until then, we'll go on learning to recognize
what we love, and what it takes
to tend what isn't for our having.
So often, fear has led me
to abandon what I know I must relinquish
in time. But for the moment,
I'll listen to her dream,
and she to mine, our mutual hearing calling
more and more detail into the light
of a joint and fragile keeping.

Holly Wren Spaulding

PRIMITIVE OBJECTS

Sleeping an hour later than usual,
the sweat smell of his neck,

coffee, even the dregs, and brine
as the tide came in. Harbor seals

then whole oceans of gold light,
his illness on the mend, Earth

thawing again, a beginning in the way
we touched each other's bodies.

Like archaeologists, how we dug
and removed by spoonfuls, layer

after layer of dirt. How it was up to us—
with small brushes, bare hands—

to save what we'd found.

Donna Hilbert

RIBOLLITA

I praise the way you save
stale bread left on the shelf too long,
rinds of Parmesan tough to grate,
old greens not crisp enough
for salad, but fine for soup
re-boiled from what's on hand.
I love the way you salvage
bruised tomato, sprouting onion,
imperfect squash, laying no morsel
to mold, nothing to waste,
filling each space with aroma
of soup, saying supper, manga!
come eat, come safely, come home.

Ada Limón

JOINT CUSTODY

Why did I never see it for what it was:
abundance. Two families, two different
kitchen tables, two sets of rules, two
creeks, two highways, two stepparents
with their fish tanks or eight tracks or
cigarette smoke or expertise in recipes or
reading skills. I cannot reverse it, the record
scratched and stopping to that original
chaotic track. But let me say, I was taken
back and forth on Sundays and it was not easy
but I was loved in each place. And so I have
two brains now. Two entirely different brains.
The one that always misses where I'm not,
the one that is so relieved to finally be home.

Lucy Griffith

ATTENTION

Home—the place of attention.
Where you know that swirl in the road
marks the dust bath of a jackrabbit.
Or that a particular Canyon Wren ends
her descending aria with a startling yee-haw.

That on our longest of days,
the sun retires on the breast
of the northwest horizon
and begins a steady southern swing
to the little knoll where we mark its winter twin.

Our lives held in this gentle cup,
palmed within an arc of light.

The Place of Attention

Our homes are not always the places where we pay the most attention. We might take care of our house or apartment, but after a while, we can begin to ignore all the things that share space with us. Since coming across "Attention" by Lucy Griffith, I've been feeling much more wonder for all the signs that tell me I'm home—the ruts of our washed-out gravel driveway, certain patches of blackberries ripening, the black-eyed Susan I planted years ago finally blooming. So often we look past such small things, perhaps not thinking our daily lives are worthy of awe. Griffith urges us to bring our attention more deeply into the places we know best and see how we are "held in this gentle cup" of home, no matter what else might be going on in our lives or in the world.

Invitation for Writing and Reflection

What are the images and signs that let you know you are home? What are the daily rituals and encounters that make a place your own?

Peg Edera

HARBORS OF MIRACLE

Once in Quebec
standing on top of a picnic table
I looked out across a valley
and saw only
tree after tree
a marching army of trees
with no space or air
only constancy and
what seemed inevitability.
The lack of welcome for my kind
was a pulse
bigger than mine.
I became weightless,
unbounded,
smaller than a molecule,
untethered.

If I knew to look
for harbors of miracle
I would have found my skin walls
and blood rivers,
the pebbles of fingernails,
the still-working bellows of lungs,
the possibility of eyes
seeing the small thing
like a pinecone,

seed for a tree,
home for a bird,
maker of rain and air—
all in the palm of my hand.

Natalie Goldberg

HOME

I am thinking of the rain in New York
the driving rain over the Metropolitan Museum
and the Guggenheim and the small delicatessen
down in the Village that sells *flanken*
I am thinking of the rain making rivers by the curb
near Ohrbach's and Penn Station
the shop selling pita sandwiches
the grease and char of lamb
rotating slowly in the raining day

I am thinking of the fruit stands now
the five hundred fruit stands all over New York
I'm thinking mostly of the dark celery leaves
above the green stalks and the bright skins of oranges
I am thinking of Macy's meat department
and the Nebraska cows
of the hundred year old air in Macy's
and the green cashmere sweaters on top of the glass counter
I am remembering the way pizza smells in the streets calling
        hunger out of ourselves
I am thinking now of the Hudson River and the rain meeting it
the mist already rising over the George Washington Bridge
and the trees growing wildly on the other shore

Rebecca Baggett

CHESTNUT

I touched a chestnut sapling
in the Georgia mountains.

My friend writes of the great trees
and their vanishing,

but I have seen a young chestnut,
tender and green, rising from its ashes.

I, too, write of loss and grief,
the hollow they carve

in the chest,
but that hollow may shelter

some new thing,
a life I could not

have imagined or wished,
a life I would never

have chosen. I have seen
the chestnut rising,

luminous,
from its own bones,

from the ashes of its first life.

Zeina Azzam

HUGGING THE TREE

It was neither part of a protest
nor a statement to the world.
I simply put my arms around
a tall oak and stood in embrace,
our bodies juxtaposed.
There was no swaying: her
trunk, solid and true, felt like
an ancestor, a pillar thick
with years. Her bark scratched
my skin if I moved, so I stayed
still. It was a time to be calm
and reflect on our presence
together. To look up to the sky
and fathom the height of my
partner. To inhale the earthy
scent. To arc my grateful arms
around this strong matriarch
and whisper into the wood
my wordless secret: I have not
hugged anyone for months,
my dear tree.

Linda Hogan

HOME IN THE WOODS

Oh home in the woods,
I am here as one hungry to eat,
one with no bread
in the garden of trees
in a place where the stone wishes to blossom.
Bullets have gone to sleep
and with effort the water
flows the way it once did.
Here, in winter, there is enough
dry wood for heat
and I enter smiling, forgetting our history.
Can you bring me to the place
where pollen is now the light
and we remember the original song?
Can you keep me
here? Can you unharm me?

NOTHING WANTS TO SUFFER

after Linda Hogan

Nothing wants to suffer. Not the wind
as it scrapes itself against the cliff. Not the cliff

being eaten, slowly, by the sea. The earth does not want
to suffer the rough tread of those who do not notice it.

The trees do not want to suffer the axe, nor see
their sisters felled by root rot, mildew, rust.

The coyote in its den. The puma stalking its prey.
These, too, want ease and a tender animal in the mouth

to take their hunger. An offering, one hopes,
made quickly, and without much suffering.

The chair mourns an angry sitter. The lamp, a scalded moth.
A table, the weight of years of argument.

We know this, though we forget.

Not the shark nor the tiger, fanged as they are.
Nor the worm, content in its windowless world

of soil and stone. Not the stone, resting in its riverbed.
The riverbed, gazing up at the stars.

Least of all, the stars, ensconced in their canopy,
looking down at all of us—their offspring—

scattered so far beyond reach.

The Awe of Aliveness

In "Nothing Wants to Suffer," humans don't make an appearance until the very end when the speaker suggests we are the "offspring" of stars. That line alone is enough to generate awe for the smallness and humility we can sometimes feel on this planet. Yet the true source of wonder comes as the poem implies that everything has the potential to feel pain, including those things that we sometimes think of as inanimate objects. A deep sense of compassion seems to unfold as the speaker humanizes the wind, the cliff, and the earth itself: showing us that everything from plants and animals, soil and stones, to the very table at which we sit can feel the "weight of years of argument." If we see all the creatures and objects around us as alive, how can we not feel wonder for them, alongside the tender realization that everything and everyone we encounter is simply seeking the peace of belonging that we can so easily offer them?

Invitation for Writing and Reflection

Begin your own writing with Linda Hogan's words "Nothing wants to suffer," and see where this poignant phrase carries your own imagination. How does your view of the world change if you see everything around you as alive and capable of feeling?

THE WAY WE LOVE SOMETHING SMALL

The translucent claws of newborn mice
this pearl cast of color,
the barely perceptible
like a ghosted threshold of being:
here   not here.
The single breath we hold
on the thinnest verge of sight:
not there   there.
A curve nearly naked
an arc of almost,
a wisp of becoming
a wand—
tiny enough to change me.

Brooke McNamara

LISTEN BACK

Stay here at the precipice, quiet.
Quiet as the sun rises
over the rooftops
across the street
and the cats watch, rapt.
Quiet as the coffee deepens
its creamy sweet acidity.
How many mornings
have I woken like this, early
and called to listen
at the window of the unknown?
Sometimes it speaks to me.
Sometimes it listens back.

Michelle Wiegers

SLOW DOWN

This morning I'm so tired
from pushing myself hard,
that as I drive down this country road
I can't bring myself to go

anywhere close to the speed limit.
I feel like a silver haired lady
peeking over my steering wheel
as I creep along, letting

the cars whiz by me.
I always assume the elderly
go slowly because they're cautious,
not wanting to hit anyone

or miss the ambulance
racing down the road with siren blaring.
But maybe they've figured out
a secret that I'm still trying to learn.

What if driving slowly
is the only way
to live my best life,
to keep from running so fast

that I go right past myself?
Running by the small child inside
who seeks to fill herself with wonder,
passing up the chance for rest,

for play, to slow myself
long enough to notice
how pleasant the rain sounds
dripping onto the roof

of the house next door,
tiny wet whispers tapping
those few remaining leaves
clinging to the maple

in my backyard,
an almost silent thrumming
slowing down my weary soul.
The steady chime

of church bells ringing
in the distance, in this moment,
reminding me, I've already
been given all that I need.

Joshua Michael Stewart

NOVEMBER PRAISE

The smell of ferns and understory
after rain. The tick, tick of stove,

flame under kettle. Bing Crosby,
and not just the Christmas records.

Cooking meat slowly off the bone,
and every kind of soup and stew.

To come this close to nostalgia,
but go no further, leaving behind

the boy who wore loneliness
like boots too big for his feet.

That time of evening,
when everything turns blue

in moonlight, when darkness
has yet to consume all for itself.

Susan Varon

THE GENTLE DARK

surrounds the house, meaning no harm.
No sirens, no calls of wolves or coyotes,
no ominous rumbling of thunder.

Nothing at all to remind me
that when I step outside there's
a world waiting. I could be living

at the end, I could be the last human
standing. Hallelujah that this is not so.
Hallelujah for the gradually lightening sky,

in which I see my actual world shining
through the blinds. Not my past world,
of New York neighborhoods and friends,

but this lovely, sun-dappled world
of now, of trees and growing things.
I hold my breath a moment

and then exhale. Yes, I welcome
with open arms another sweet
and necessary day.

Jacqueline Suskin

SUNRISE, SUNSET

Nothing can keep me
from watching first light
rise over eastern mountains.
This is what makes me sit still.
Not sleep. Not a lover.
And nothing can prevent me
from soaking in the final
gift of sun as it bleeds brilliant
over the western mountains.
This is what calls me
to repeatedly walk toward the Pacific.
I have to commit to something
in this life and a flaming circle
in the sky seems right.
The best attempt at ritual
and routine, guided by light.

Joanne Durham

SUNRISE SONNET FOR MY SON

My son unloads the dishwasher first thing
each morning. I think of him, four hundred
miles away, as I stand on tiptoe to shelve
last night's wine glasses, stack my mother's
dessert plates, open the drawer beneath
the oven just deep enough for all the pots
and pans. He says for him, too, it's a kind
of meditation, this routine he and his wife
have shaped into the contours of a shared
life, fluted and spacious as the overflowing
fruit bowl. This is what he possesses, not
Lenox or Waterford, which neither of us owns,
this man I raised, who hums as he sorts
the silverware, noticing how each spoon shines.

Meghan Dunn

ODE TO BUTTER

To its sweetness and salt, to its sunshine
in a stick, spreading in sheets of gold
over a cob of summer corn, a halved
blueberry muffin, to its chameleon nature,
crisping and softening and browning
and caramelizing everything it touches.
To the sound its waxed paper wrapper makes
when a knife is sliced through at the blue line.
Satisfying. To the friend who once answered,
Well, do you want it to be good? when I asked
if this much butter was enough and who watched
without judgment, with motherly approval
as I sliced in more and then more. To the way
it goes "straight to my thighs," themselves butter-
like in their softness, their pleasingly elastic firmness,
the way they too spread, golden, are sweet
and salty. To the sound they make swishing together.
Satisfying. This permission I give myself.

Robbi Nester

ROT

The garbage reeks, full of leftovers
and moldy lemons, mats of dryer lint,
like a skin of algae on the surface
of a pond. I ought to take the full bag
out, but I'm reluctant to engage with
the decay that's at the heart of everything.
And yet, if one could study it impartially,
without a trace of terror or repulsion,
the vivid shades of dissolution rival
the desert after rain, spilled paint
spreading to the far horizon. Even
the odors hover on the edge of almost
beautiful, as full as perfume's ripe musk,
purple as the jacaranda. It can even
be delicious—at least to some. Consider
the fragrant funk of some ripe cheeses,
durian, or kimchi, thousand-year-old eggs,
buried in the yard until the yolk marbles
greenish black. Without rot, none of us
could thrive. Everything that grows
feeds on what went before, ocean reefs
seeded by a wealth of putrid whalefall,
ancient cities stacked one atop another,
rising from the same foundation, fertile
ground for everything to come.

Naomi Shihab Nye

LITTLE FARMER

With love, to Earthdance Farm

She pulled us up the hill in a red wagon.
We rolled home with brown sacks in our laps.
Later I worked at Mueller's Organic Farm,
the rows knew my step.
I plucked berries gently, never bruising.
They paid 5 cents a box, it felt like a lot.
All my life has had that light, square shape.
Such ruddy sunstruck pride
in the farmers named Al and Caroline,
Al loved his mounds of squash, sacks of beans,
with fierce intensity. Caroline said *Nope, I only
love him.* Their okra bore an essence of perfection,
ripe corn whispered inside its perfect sheaves
and drifty web of hair. *You are here,* it said.
You will always be here. Years later Al told me,
Your mother was the most lovely person
who ever walked up my drive, that long shiny
ponytail, those huge eyes. She asked
the best questions. That shows intelligence.
He sang me songs, lost love and lonely stars.
I had never known he played a guitar.
Why didn't I ask more questions?
The lives spun out. He wanted me to stay.

I wish I could harvest his patience
from fifty years away. Al long dead,
his dutiful Caroline dead, their farm still
a farm though, one victory! I'd tell him
how right he was about slowness,
the path of sunlight through leaves,
how dirt has always befriended me,
birdcalls beyond,
how his shy smile, waving goodbye with a hoe,
stayed with me forever, how no tomato
was ever better than the one he held in his hand.

James Crews

TOMATOES

When I bite into the bruise-
colored flesh of this heirloom tomato
known as a Cherokee Purple,
I'm transported back to the dirt road
that ran along the Meramec River
where my father pulled over
at the farm stand, then stepped out
of the truck, brushed for a moment
in gravel dust suspended in the sun.
He came back grinning, gripping
a bag of homegrown Beefsteaks so fat
they were already bursting their juices
through the brown paper, running
down his long-gone hands, which I am
reaching out to touch again before
he turns the key in the ignition,
begging him not to go, not just yet,
as I salt the next slice.

Sarah Wolfson

WHAT I LIKE ABOUT BEANS

That sure way, after they unfurl
from their tiny selves, the plants retain
a flap of former life: the seed relic
sliding down the stalk, lower and
lower, a set of not-quite wings
and not-quite leaves. How even after
the now brown casing has dropped
to earth as compost, the bean itself
remains as two naked curls
of cellulose, a little shriveled,
a lot misshapen, but still
for all the world a set of small
animated hands about to clap
for all the green that outstrips them.

Susan Musgrave

TOMATOES ON THE WINDOWSILL
AFTER RAIN

and bread by the woodstove
waiting to be punched down again.
I step out into the dark
morning, find the last white flowers
in a Mason jar by the door
and a note from a friend saying
he would call again later. I go back
into the kitchen, tomatoes
on the windowsill after rain,
small things but vast
if you desire them.

The deep fresh red.
This life rushing towards me.

Mary Jo LoBello Jerome

TOMATO INTUITION

God made me this way, and I don't dispute it. Amen.
—Flannery O'Connor

The cherry tomatoes sprawl and bury every other plant. God,
they're tireless. The peppers, chard, eggplants, beets made

into involuntary supports, smothered. New hairy stems daze me
each day like Jack's magic stalk. So dizzying, their reach. This

garden, planned in neat rows, now a fecund tangle. The way
I've been taught to tie-back or prune branches is useless. And I

finally surrender the need for control. The vines don't
hold back. Flower and fruit overflow. Who could dispute

these sweet and acid gifts to the tongue? Such a luscious mess. It
is time to give thanks for the persistent, the genuine, amen.

Leah Naomi Green

CARROT

Take all summer,
your ember

from the sun,
its walking meditation.

Store it in small
vaults of light

to keep
the rest of us

when winter seals
around each day.

We'll flicker
to the table.

We'll gather
to your orange flame.

Nothing for Granted

I love poems that take the most ordinary things and transform them into something worthy of wonder, using only the power of the writer's close attention. "Carrot" is a short, deceptively simple poem that does just that as it imagines a carrot in the ground, stoking its "ember from the sun" all summer long. Though I'd never thought about how the inside of a carrot looks, Leah Naomi Green shows us up close those "small vaults of light," which still contain summer's brightness and heat. She also imagines the light of the sun as a kind of "walking meditation" passing across the garden, reminding us of the slow yet miraculous process of growth and renewal by which we are all fed.

Invitation for Writing and Reflection

Choose some humble, seemingly ordinary thing and write a poem (perhaps a kind of ode) addressed to it. You might choose as your subject something that you particularly love but that others might find too plain or simple to be worthy of amazement.

Jessica Gigot

AMENDS

It is hard to hold a homegrown
      head of broccoli in your hand
and not feel proud.
Seed to start,

seedling to robust stalk and floret,
I cradle this broccoli like my first born.

The infant I protected from damping-off,
      aphids, club root, and pesky flea beetles
         dotting up all the leaves.

The green gleams and sparkles.
In that one hour on that one day

I made amends with the earth.

Other times, I buy the shipped-in stuff,
      California's wellspring
touched by a thousand hands
      and automated sanitation.

Sweat makes this one something special—
      the give and take of it all,
         my muddied pride.

Lahab Assef Al-Jundi

WHAT THE ROSES SAID TO ME

Don't forget me!
Always remember
my beauty is for your eyes.
My fragrance is for your spirit.
My unfolding
is my invitation to you
to yield to your own.

When your skies seem darkest,
when your heart is gripped by pain,
when uncertainty and fear
creep into your days,
come back to me.
Come into me.
Camp between my scented sheets.
Let me show you
a passageway back
to love.

Rage Hezekiah

LAYERS

after Seamus Heaney

All the lemons lit in the kitchen bowl
seem softened by the sun, whose morning lull

illuminates your hands splayed
open on the butcher block table.

Oh, what you can make with your hands,
and how I ache to witness

your wooden spoon mixing six
simple ingredients in a ceramic vessel.

Bake me a cake again. Place squash blossoms
and nasturtium on the plate,

spread the pastry with sweet cream,
a meditative motion, slow and serene.

Mamma, once you made such gentle things.

Dorianne Laux

MY MOTHER'S COLANDER

Holes in the shape of stars
punched in gray tin, dented,
cheap, beaten by each
of her children with a wooden spoon.

Noodle catcher, spaghetti stopper,
pouring cloudy rain into the sink,
swirling counter clockwise
down the drain, starch slime
on the backside, caught
in the piercings.

Scrubbed for sixty years, packed
and unpacked, the baby's
helmet during the cold war,
a sinking ship in the bathtub,
little boat of holes.

Dirt scooped in with a plastic
shovel, sifted to make cakes
and castles. Wrestled
from each other's hands,
its tin feet bent and re-bent.

Bowl daylight fell through
onto freckled faces, noon stars
on the pavement, the universe
we circled aiming jagged stones,
rung bells it caught and held.

Sue Ann Gleason

ASK ME

Ask me for the measure of starter
and water in a loaf of sourdough bread.
How to gently pull the dough across
the surface of a marble slab, folding
it like an envelope so that the gluten
strengthens slowly and with intention.

Ask me how those loaves of sourdough
kept my hands steady and my mind
occupied on days that fear and anxiety
rose as exponentially as the starter.

Ask me about my grandmother's kitchen.
The sound of onions sizzling in a cast iron skillet,
the smell of garlic, the shape of her hands
chopping vegetables, teasing pie crust over heaps
of cinnamon soaked apples.

Ask me about candles on countertops,
how she lit those candles daily and prayed
to patron saints, the depth of her faith reflected
in the whisper-thin pages of her prayer book
and the seven children she raised in the midst
of The Great Depression.

Ask me about the sound of her voice praying
the rosary in Italian and how that became
a lullaby singing me to sleep. Ask me
about breakfast in her home, thick slabs
of toasted bread slathered
with cinnamon butter and smiles.

Ask me about my grandfather's breakfast—
the crunch of cornflakes, the tap, tap, tap of spoon
on the delicate shell of a soft-boiled egg.
How he swirled the remaining milk in the bowl
with the last drop of thick, dark coffee from his cup.
And, if my memory serves me here, a shot of whiskey
to warm his belly for a day digging ditches,
the price he paid to live in America.

Ask about the garden out back, how in summer months
it resembles the one my grandfather tended—
sun ripened tomatoes, basil and beans.
How every morsel in my kitchen, from sourdough
loaves to the slow simmer of tomato sauce,
is the love language of my grandmother's hands.

Paola Bruni

THE LESSON

On Sundays, Grandmother alight on the altar
of making and I, only old enough to kneel
on a wooden chair beside her, watched.
From the cupboard, she unearthed a dusky
pastry board, flour formed into a heaping crater,
the center hollowed. Eggs, white as doves. Salt.
Cup of milk, fragrant and simple. No spatula.
No bowl or mixer. Just a pastry board
and Grandmother's naked, calcified fingers
proclaiming each ingredient into the next.
She murmured into the composition
until the dough fattened, perspired, grew
under her ravenous eye. A rolling pin
to create a still, quiet surface. Then, the point
of a sharp knife chiseling flags of wide golden noodles.
For days, the fettuccini draped from wooden
clothing racks in her bedroom under the scrutiny
of Jesus and his Mother. Mornings, I slipped
into Grandmother's bed, dreamt about eating noodles
swathed in butter and the sauce of a hundred
ripe tomatoes roasted on the fire.

Meghan Sterling

CHICKADEE

My daughter sang softly this morning,
respecting the sleep of others like a little nun,
whispering her vespers to the dolls she cradled
on a pillow in the middle of the kitchen floor.
I savored her quiet, her voice like wings, delicate
as branch-tips just beginning to crown with buds.
Her song was the black throat of a chickadee,
hopping from limb to limb, crested by blue sky
like all the love that had been waiting
once I stopped searching and started looking.
But that's the way the sky is. Always there,
but still, a revelation on a spring morning
when all is quiet enough to hear it hum.
Suppose I had decided to stay childless?
I'd be listening to the birds on the lines,
desperate to find anything to make me feel
as tender as my daughter so easily does,
singing in hushed tones to her monkey and owl
wrapped in a blanket of old towels.

Faith Shearin

MY DAUGHTER DESCRIBES THE TARANTULA

Her voice is as lovely and delicate as a web.
She describes how fragile they are,
how they can die from a simple fall.
Then she tells me about their burrows
which are tidy and dry and decorated
with silk. They are solitary, she tells me,
and utterly mild, and when they are
threatened they fling their hairs, trying
not to bite. She says they are most
vulnerable when they molt: unable
to eat for days while they change.
They are misunderstood, she explains,
and suddenly her description becomes
personal. She wants to keep one
as a pet, to appreciate it properly,
to build it a place where it belongs.

Laura Foley

LOST AND FOUND

On my sophomore science field trip
to the rocky Maine coast,
I sat captivated by a tidal pool, a little village
of crawling crabs, snails, starfish darting,
a sea anemone appearing to sing.
I stayed so long, I forgot the rising tide,
my teachers, classmates waiting
on the bus. On the exam,
I couldn't calculate the pitch of waves,
or chemical composition of anything,
but I knew how to lose myself
in the world of tiny shifting things.

Joy Harjo

REDBIRD LOVE

We watched her grow up.
She was the urgent chirper,
Fledgling flier.
And when spring rolled
Out its green
She'd grown
Into the most noticeable
Bird-girl.
Long-legged and just
The right amount of blush
Tipping her wings, crest
And tail, and
She knew it
in the bird parade.
We watched her strut.
She owned her stuff.
The males perked their armor, greased their wings,
And flew sky-loop missions
To show off
For her.
In the end
There was only one.
There's that one you circle back to—for home.

This morning
The young couple scavenge seeds
On the patio.
She is thickening with eggs.
Their minds are busy with sticks the perfect size, tufts of fluff
Like dandelion, and other pieces of soft.
He steps aside for her, so she can eat.
Then we watch him fill his beak
Walk tenderly to her and kiss her with seed.
The sacred world lifts up its head
To notice—
We are double, triple blessed.

Kim Stafford

WREN'S NEST IN A SHED NEAR AURORA

Three tiny eggs in thistledown
cupped in a swirl of grass
in the pocket of the tool belt
I hung on the wall of the shed
when it finally stood complete—
will be three songs
offering local dignity for
my country enthralled by war
in distant lands.
           Stand back
cautiously, close the door
tenderly, let the future
ripen, grow wings,
and build songs.

Sharon Corcoran

ENCOUNTER

The red plastic dish, perforated
with beak-sized holes, decorated
with yellow petals feigning flowers,
dangles from my hand. In it,
sweetened water. As I carry it
toward the stand where it will hang,
some force, invisible at first
but fierce—a delicate wind
against my hand, perhaps—
stops me. I look down
and a small green body hovers,
her beak at the petaled opening,
inches from my hand, my heart.
Her fearlessness and minute fury
overcome me. Every beam in me
is focused on this—the humbling honor
bestowed, being allowed to wait
upon this tiny god.

José A. Alcántara

ARCHILOCHUS COLUBRIS

The hummingbirds have arrived,
beating their invisible wings beyond the window
where buds are beginning to break.

They come bearing the light of Panama,
Colombia, Costa Rica, the red fire of the tropics,
here, to this mountain, still spotted in snow.

I go out among them, in my red coat,
hoping they will mistake me for a flower.
They buzz close, hovering before my face.

If only one of them would touch me, I would
sprout feathers and take to the air, my wings
tracing infinity, my throat turning to rubies.

Emilie Lygren

MEDITATION

Sitting near the window,
I watched a fly stammering
against the glass,
trying to break free
and transcend the
transparent boundary
it could not comprehend.

As I cupped my hands around the fly
then let it out the open door,
I wished that we could trade places—

that someone would gently remove me
from the invisible walls
I have pressed myself up against,
offer an opening I am too small to see.

After sitting longer,
I start to think that maybe I am all parts of the story—

the trembling fly,
the gently cupped hands,
the clear glass window,
the necessary air outside.

Margaret Hasse

ART

As the sun begins to build its house of gold
an artist is called to her window.
Alone in the attic of creation
free to leave her body, lift bird-like
and settle on bare branches,
she can portray what is before,
within or beyond herself.
With pencil, paper, color,
she paints an upside-down bowl
of blue essence some call heaven.
Anne Frank, too, in the bolt-hole
of a tiny annex found her patch
of sky and shared her vision.
She wrote in her diary: *Think*
of all the beauty in yourself and
everything around you and be happy.

Mark Nepo

ART LESSON

The mind moves like a pencil.
The heart moves like a brush.

While the mind can draw
exquisite prints, the heart
with its deep bright colors
will ignore the lines.

If you only follow your mind,
you will never go outside the lines.

If you only follow your heart,
what you touch will never
resemble anything.

We must be
a student of both.

For the mind can build
itself a home, but only
the heart can live in it.

Cristina M. R. Norcross

BREATHING PEACE

If peace was something we could hold
in our hands,
we would mold it like clay.
We would shape it into a circle,
leaving our thumbprint on it,
then carefully pass it into
the knowing hands of the next person,
as if handling a newborn sparrow.

If peace was something we could breathe,
we would close our eyes and savor the precious air
flowing into our lungs—
passing through our lips.
That exhale would be a prayer.
It would be a song in three-part harmony.

If peace was something we could taste,
it would be figs drizzled with honey.
We would arrange it on a plate
with a silk-petaled sunflower
decorating the center.
We would pass the plate around
with reverence, ensuring that every single person
received nourishment.

If peace was something we could walk to,
it would be a sacred labyrinth of circles.
We would greet each other on the meditative path.
We would come together at the center
and admire our cohesive union—
arms raised to the sun,
rejoicing in what we could not see or touch,
but we could feel it.
We have been walking together
for such a long time.
We have always been at peace,
but we become lost in the forgetting.

Caroline Webster

EXPECTING

I wait sometimes
for hours, days, nine months
for an idea,
a first line,
or simply one word.

I wait so long I never start.

The stories, though, are there.
Aren't they?
Gestating, always awaiting birth.

I must prod gently,
nurture,
ease them out.

That is peace,
I think,
delivering
what emerges.

Mark Nepo

THE CLEARING

I had climbed beyond what
I knew, in search of something
lasting, and far away from the
crowd, I found this clearing
from which I glimpsed life
outside of my own story.

And life was never more
revealing, though I couldn't
stay there, any more than a
bird can nest in the sun.

So, I came back into the
world, though I'm never far
from that clearing. I carry it
within like a candle lit from
the great unending fire.

And when exhausted of my
thoughts, I find the clearing in
your quiet breathing as you sleep,
in the song that parts everyone's
trouble, in the moment the old
painter lifts his brush from the
canvas.

Even in these words I leave
on the page like ripples
in the water.

Laura Foley

WHAT STILLNESS

Lily pads ripple in summer breeze,
as if they bloomed for me,
revelation-white clouds float
through a divine blue sky.
No human voices break
the stillness of this hilltop pond
where I come to forget
the foolishness of homo sapiens—
where a trout leaps from the lake,
splashes shining down,
opening a glimpse into
the world below the surface.
My dog, wet from her swim
between the visible and the hidden,
shakes dots of sparkling light
from her dark coat,
forming a watery aura.
What sunlight does to water,
stillness does to us.

The Gift of Stillness

As much as I value downtime, especially when spent in nature, I still resist the stillness I most need in order to glimpse, as Laura Foley puts it, "the world below the surface" of our stressful lives. Foley's meditative poem "What Stillness" offers the gift of pointing out what we can do when we start to feel restless or stressed: Find a peaceful place, perhaps like her hilltop pond, where we can go and be quiet, simply reflecting on what's directly around us. Slowly then— and it always takes more time than we'd like—the world opens back up to us, and each cloud turns "revelation-white," as we see the value of a short break from human voices and the "foolishness" of our species, too often bent on harming each other and our planet. Spaces like these, separate from the bustle and noise of crowds and news, are necessary for renewal as they allow our minds and bodies to settle. Only then might we see again the "sparkling light" of water shaken from a dog's coat and be reminded of the small miracles that make life worth living.

Invitation for Writing and Reflection

Find a place like the one Foley describes in the poem, even if it is simply a quiet corner in your home or a bench in a local park. Stay still for a few moments and see what calls to you from that place "between the visible and the hidden."

Lisa Zimmerman

LAKE AT NIGHT

No whales tonight but the moon
sings their music, a net of light
pulling the wind
into blue slopes.

The trees, with their nests
of new leaves, move invisibly
toward shore. The air
is sharp and tangy as seaweed.

Long after dark we hear
fish rise out of the water,
their scales studded
with tiny barnacles,
their joy bigger
than their bodies.

Joseph Bruchac

BIRDFOOT'S GRAMPA

The old man
must have stopped our car
two dozen times to climb out
and gather into his hands
the small toads blinded
by our lights and leaping,
live drops of rain.

The rain was falling,
a mist about his white hair
and I kept saying
you can't save them all
accept it, get back in,
we've got places to go.

But, leathery hands full
of wet brown life
knee deep in the summer
roadside grass
he just smiled and said
they have places to go
too.

Heather Swan

BOY

He burst from the cattails
clutching a bullfrog—
the glabrous body
slick with mud,
thick legs outstretched,
but somehow tranquil.
His hands could easily crush
this creature whose soft belly
is the color of milk,
who can breathe
through her skin,
whose only protections
are a transparent eyelid
and quickness.

This is the child who,
in the darkness, unable
to sleep, curls into
the body he came from
and asks, *But who invented war?*
And, *Can a bullet go through brick?*
Can a bullet go through steel?

Now, at the water's edge,
filled with a wild holiness,
he navigates the balance,
then lets the frog go.

Nikita Gill

YOUR SOFT HEART

You are still the child who gently places
Fallen baby birds back in their nests.
You are still the soft soul that gets
Your heart broken over cruel words
And awful acts when you watch the news.
You are still the gentle heart who once
Tried to heal a flower by attempting to stick
Its petals back on when ignorant feet trampled it.

This is why you are important.
This is why you will always be needed.

Kindness is the greatest endangered thing.
And here you are, existing, your heart so full with it.

Joyce Sutphen

FROM OUT THE CAVE

When you have been
at war with yourself
for so many years that
you have forgotten why,
when you have been driving
for hours and only
gradually begin to realize
that you have lost the way,
when you have cut
hastily into the fabric,
when you have signed
papers in distraction,
when it has been centuries
since you watched the sun set
or the rain fall, and the clouds,
drifting overhead, pass as flat
as anything on a postcard;
when, in the midst of these
everyday nightmares, you
understand that you could
wake up,

you could turn
and go back
to the last thing you
remember doing
with your whole heart:
that passionate kiss,
the brilliant drop of love
rolling along the tongue of a green leaf,
then you wake,
you stumble from your cave,
blinking in the sun,
naming every shadow
as it slips.

Marilyn McCabe

WEB

Lately everything is

astounding me,
miles of phone lines,

garage door openers,

spatulas,
my shoes.

What is the way

to pay tribute to glory?
The aspen knows:

applause with every breeze.

How best to enflame
the holy fire?

Light
is on my face

filtered through glowing leaves.
Around my feet

a tumble of extraordinary
rocks pocked, striated

pink, gold. A frenzy

of riverdrops,
riot of current.

One spider is rapidly

tying me here,
its lines like spokes

to a spinning wheel.

We are silver,
quivering.

Anne Evans

A NEW VARIANT

They say a new variant has been detected.
Have you heard about it?
Wildly contagious, it is believed
to infect the mind's eye.

They say it jams the brain
and may weaken your old opinions.
The machine of your mind
may stop chattering and start to hum.

They say the variant has a side effect—
compassion. Many report tearfulness, a tender heart,
empathy for the stranger with 20 items in the quick check line
or the guy following too close in traffic.

They say it will loosen your grip on your judgments
and create space for curiosity. In fact,
you might be rendered mute by all you do not know.
And, for sure, your immunity to wonder will be broken down.

This variant, they say, will make you dizzy, distract you
with the possibilities for simple kindness. You could
lose your place in line, even forget why you're waiting,
angry and afraid, in the first place.

Barbara Crooker

THIS SUMMER DAY

That sprinkler is at it again,
hissing and spitting its arc
of silver, and the parched
lawn is tickled green. The air
hums with the busy traffic
of butterflies and bees,
who navigate without lane
markers, stop signs, directional
signals. One of my friends
says we're now in the shady
side of the garden, having moved
past pollination, fruition,
and all that bee-buzzed jazz,
into our autumn days. But I say wait.
It's still summer, and the breeze is full
of sweetness spilled from a million petals;
it wraps around your arms, lifts the hair
from the back of your neck.
The salvia, coreopsis, roses
have set the borders on fire,
and the peaches waiting to be picked
are heavy with juice. We are still ripening
into our bodies, still in the act of becoming.
Rejoice in the day's long sugar.
Praise that big fat tomato of a sun.

Ted Kooser

A GLINT

I watched a glint of morning sunlight
climbing a thread of spider's silk
in a gentle breeze. It shinnied up
from the tip of a dewy stalk of grass
to an overhanging branch, then
disappeared into the leaves. But soon
another followed, and then another,
glint after glint, and though they made
no sound, what I could see was music,
not melody but one clear, shining note
plucked over and over, as if the sun
were tuning the day, then handing it
to me so I could be the one to play it.

Derek Sheffield

FOR THOSE WHO WOULD SEE

the swift and ceaseless sprinkler whirling
and flinging its bright globes

drop by drop has filled a blue bowl
left out on the lawn. The little pool
formed by that embrace never stops

breaking and regathering—winks of calm
coming between bouts of splattering—

and in the way the pool accepts
each troubling drop so it becomes
the surface that in the next instant

shatters at the next and so on,
this is also clearly a matter of light

splashed and light
scattered in all directions
for anyone who happens to be watching.

REFLECTIVE PAUSE

Winks of Calm

I can't help but read "For Those Who Would See" as a commentary on the nature of our minds, the way our thoughts and worries come and go with only "winks of calm" in between bouts of distraction and disturbance. At first glance, Derek Sheffield's poem offers something mundane and simple: "a blue bowl left out on the lawn," filled with water from the "swift and ceaseless sprinkler." Yet in Sheffield's masterful hands, this act of truly *seeing* the blue bowl, the "bright globes" of water, and the sprinkler itself becomes an exercise in mindfulness and guided attention. He doesn't simply describe the bowl of water, but instead shows us how its surface (like that of the mind) is always "breaking and regathering." What's different about this "little pool" is that it "accepts each troubling drop" without resistance, adding it to the whole. By watching exactly what happens in this scene and allowing his observations to ripple outward with meaning, the speaker implies that so much of life is not about what we see, but how we *choose* to see whatever crosses our path.

Invitation for Writing and Reflection

What calms you in your world right now, even if it's something very simple? Can you describe the effect of this object or person on you? Can you make a whole list of things that have offered you those "winks of calm" lately?

Sally Bliumis-Dunn

AUBADE

You call it the jeweling hour,
these miniature glistening globes

all over the pines—
like a glass bead necklace

left on a woman's dresser
that cannot possibly tell the tale

of what happened before
the tousled bed lay empty.

With a little wind or sun
the water droplets

will disappear from the trees
and you and I will cut

the peaches for our cereal, read
the paralyzing headlines in the paper,

but for now, their glister
dangles on the branches

from last night's rain that held
the house in its wild pounding

Kim Stafford

ADVICE FROM A RAINDROP

You think you're too small
to make a difference? Tell me
about it. You think you're
helpless, at the mercy of forces
beyond your control? Been there.

Think you're doomed to disappear,
just one small voice among millions?
That's no weakness, trust me. That's
your wild card, your trick, your
implement. They won't see you coming

until you're there, in their faces, shining,
festive, expendable, eternal. Sure you're
small, just one small part of a storm that
changes everything. That's how you win,
my friend, again and again and again.

Danusha Laméris

LET RAIN BE RAIN

Let rain be rain.
      Let wind be wind.
Let the small stone
      be the small stone.

May the bird
    rest on its branch,
the beetle in its burrow.

May the pine tree
    lay down its needles.
The rockrose, its petals.

It's early. Or it's late.
    The answers
to our questions
    lie hidden
in acorn, oyster, the seagull's
    speckled egg.

We've come this far, already.
    Why not let breath
be breath. Salt be salt.

How faithful the tide
    that has carried us—
that carries us now—
      out to sea
    and back.

Nina Bagley

GATHERING

We are gatherers,
the ones who pick up sticks and stones
and old wasp nests fallen by the
door of the barn,
walnuts with holes that look like
eyes of owls,
bits of shell not whole but lovely
in their brokenness,
we are the ones who bring home
empty eggs of birds,
and place them on a small glass shelf,
to keep for what? How long?
It matters not. What matters
is the gathering,
the pockets filled with remnants
of a day evaporated, the traces of
certain memory, a lingering smell,
a smile that came with the shell.

Stuart Kestenbaum

HOLDING THE LIGHT

Gather up whatever is
glittering in the gutter,
whatever has tumbled
in the waves or fallen
in flames out of the sky,

for it's not only our
hearts that are broken,
but the heart
of the world as well.
Stitch it back together.

Make a place where
the day speaks to the night
and the earth speaks to the sky.
Whether we created God
or God created us

it all comes down to this:
In our imperfect world
we are meant to repair
and stitch together
what beauty there is, stitch it

with compassion and wire.
See how everything
we have made gathers
the light inside itself
and overflows? A blessing.

Alberto Ríos

THE BROKEN

Something is always broken.
Nothing is perfect longer than a day—
Every roof has a broken tile,
Every mouth a chipped tooth.
Something is always broken
But the world endures the break:
The broken twig is how we follow the trail.
The broken promise is the one we remember.
Something changed is pushed out the door,
Sad, perhaps, but ready, too ready, for the world.
Something is always broken.
Something is always fixed.

Alfred K. LaMotte

GENTLE

A gentler world begins
in the way you touch your heart.
Be soft with the light inside you.
Caress your body with this breath.
God is nothing else
but the place where the sun comes up
in your chest.
You are the glimmering destination.
You are the golden honey daubed
on the bread of the ordinary.
Whatever is perfect,
whatever is heavenly,
begins here.

Patricia Clark

CREED

I believe in one body, ligaments almighty, skin
wrapping the thankful bones, and the resurrection
of the stomach, waking to hunger each day

with dreams of basil and butter, fennel, old gouda
cheese, and wine poured like sunlight into glass.
I believe in the fretting of shadow and sun

on backyard grass, in the shedding of the oak,
in the temptation of an umbrella on the deck,
a table, a chair, and an opened book.

The ascension into light, especially after lying down
with another, causes us to sit at the right
hand of whatever spirit guides us, called love

by some believers. And I believe in perennials,
bark, moss instead of grass, the pollen stuck
on a stamen, the hyssop turning blue as the night.

Michael Simms

SOMETIMES I WAKE EARLY

Sometimes I wake early and walk through the house
touching doors that swing into darkness
my bare toes searching out
toys and magazines.

Outside it might be raining, a full wind
filling the trees like sails. I sit
in the love seat under the bay window, hugging
myself, letting the children's dreams wash over me
like waves.

Last night we took a friend for a walk along the edge
of our mountain. She looked out
over the city, the rivers, the sultry slopes
crowded with sumac and maple
and said *So you know where you live.*

Yes, in the darkness and rain
our small house stands in a huddle of houses
under the clouds, in a story
we ourselves are telling.

Marjorie Moorhead

HEAD IN THE CLOUDS

The cloud, so distant from me here,
on earth, on this wood of our deck,
on two feet, looking up.
I reel it in, and imagine
droplets misting my face . . .
tears or shower; relief, renewal;
it's all there, in a white fluffy ball
changing semblance in winds
that come from all directions.
Able to morph, adapt.
Can I be the cloud? May I
take it as my cotton-filled pillow,
tuck it under my head,
let muscles relax,
and dream-visions come?
I send thoughts up and away.
Near, and far; supportive, and sieve-like,
I will bring cloud down, wrap it round,
wear it as a shawl, or skirt. I will twirl,
letting cloud take what shapes it may.
I know there are days I laugh aloud,
and in some, feel enveloped by trepidation.
Let me remember, while still free from shroud,
to lift my gaze and not ignore.
In that space and time, of each given day,
whichever season, let me adore,
adore, adore.

Joseph Fasano

LETTER

Tonight, as you walk out
into the stars, or the forest, or the city,
look up
as you must have looked
before love came,
before love went,
before ash was ash.
Look at them: the city's
mists, the winters.
And the moon's glass
you must have held once
in the beginning.
That new moon
you must have touched once
in the waters,
saying *change me, change*
me, change me. All I want
is to be more of what I am.

Penny Harter

JUST GRAPEFRUIT

Carefully, I place half a grapefruit
into the small white bowl that fits it
perfectly, use the brown-handled
serrated knife to cut around the rim,
separate the sections.

The first bite is neither sweet nor bitter,
but I drag a drop or two of honey around
the top, love how it glazes each pink piece,
then seeps between dividing membranes.

Pale seeds pop up from their snug burial
in the center hole, and when I'm finished,
I squeeze sticky juice from the spent rind
and drink it down.

Each grapefruit is an offering, its bright
flesh startling my fasting tongue. When
bitterness spills from the morning news,
I temper it with grapefruit, savor hidden
gifts as I slice it open, free each glistening
segment, and enter honeyed grapefruit time.

Jane Kenyon

IN SEVERAL COLORS

Every morning, cup of coffee
in hand, I look out at the mountain.
Ordinarily, it's blue, but today
it's the color of an eggplant.

And the sky turns
from gray to pale apricot
as the sun rolls up
Main Street in Andover.

I study the cat's face
and find a trace of white
around each eye, as if
he made himself up today
for a part in the opera.

Kathryn Petruccelli

INSTINCT

My cat loves sweat, loves
to tuck the leather patch
of her nose into the space
under my arm, run
her rough-tab tongue along
my neck, flesh glistening
after a brisk walk, craves
nothing more than to taste
salt of exertion,
sometimes even to take
a small bite. What it would be
to have such freedom—
to step into our desires
as if they were owed us,
our faces pressed up against
that which we cannot control.
We'd sniff here and there
for the thing to stir our blood,
and, on finding it, plunge forward
without thought for consequence—
not in wanton greed—
but sure-footed
along trajectories that ignite—
all that surrounds us aglow
in the light of a contented sky.
What kind of world would it be?

Each of us moving to rhythms
passed on by previous purveyors
of stardust, grown in the fat
of our marrow, ancient
knowledge from the whole
of who we are that drives
not toward money,
obligation, fear,
but toward joy and abandon,
instinct, impulse, wonder.

Terri Kirby Erickson

GOLDFINCH

Stunned by an unforgiving
pane of glass, a finch
fell to the ground
like a splash of pale
yellow paint. It sat
shivering in the snow,
its heartbeat faster
than a spinning bobbin
in the aftermath of such
a killing blow. Yet,
this little bird's thimble-
full of life held fast
to its fragile body,
and was soon cradled
by a loving human hand.
There, with splayed
feathers stroked smooth,
belly warmed by
a kind woman's skin,
the goldfinch rallied.
It spread its gilded wings
and flew to a snow-
laden branch, forgetting
before it got there,

the sky's unyielding
reflection—then flew
again—a bird-shaped
star with billions
of years left to burn.

Ada Limón

IT'S THE SEASON I OFTEN MISTAKE

Birds for leaves, and leaves for birds.
The tawny yellow mulberry leaves
are always goldfinches tumbling
across the lawn like extreme elation.
The last of the maroon crabapple
ovates are song sparrows that tremble
all at once. And today, just when I
could not stand myself any longer,
a group of field sparrows, that were
actually field sparrows, flew up into
the bare branches of the hackberry
and I almost collapsed: leaves
reattaching themselves to the tree
like a strong spell for reversal. What
else did I expect? What good
is accuracy amidst the perpetual
scattering that unspools the world.

Katherine J. Williams

LATE AUGUST, LAKE CHAMPLAIN

The longer I sit, the louder they become,
the offerings of this pale morning.
No blare of birdsong, no display of light
to play through night's watery leavings.
Neither chill nor warmth—I'm aware of being
aware of the seamless air.
But the tone of an unknown bird tickles the silence.
Spiderwebs wink in invisible wind.
Beyond the trees, vast lungs of unseen water breathe.
The ferry's wail floats through a muffling cloud.
Almost hidden in the green tangle of maple and beech,
A single red leaf.

Laura Ann Reed

FORTITUDE

Twelve leaves,
all that remains
of the maple's autumn conflagration,
flutter in a chill breeze.
At the tree's base lie the fallen,
shrunken, withered,
their glorious red now the brown of earth
into whose depths they sink and decompose—
their atoms and molecules
the warp and weave
of next spring's flags of victory.
But these dozen leaves,
these flaming angels,
their beauty terrifies.
They spin and turn in wind,
unyielding. I'm consumed
by their magnificence.
I bow to them, sing their praises,
pray to them for courage,
fortitude, protection
from my human uncertainties.

Nathan Spoon

POEM OF THANKFULNESS

Today I am thankful for morning frost
touched by sunlight and sparkling

on lawns and fields   I am thankful too
for you and the warmth provided to my feet

inside ordinary socks and shoes and the way
the music of your voice enters my ears

and warms my heart leaving this planet of ours
spinning (if only slightly) more easily;

and I will consider how the world is good
difficult and good and how a lifetime

is both too short and too long
and how the injured heart cannot heal but

as researchers in Sweden have discovered
the muscle of our disadvantaged organ also can

and does slowly replenish itself   Today
when the bigness of the sky asks whoever

is standing beneath it are you ready
the gray trees drowsing and temporarily losing

the last of their burnt sienna leaves will say yes
and you will say yes and I will say yes too

Annie Lighthart

LET THIS DAY

Let this day born in sackcloth and ashes
shift. Let it change, rearrange. Let it come back
made new and barking, snout pushed to table
with joy. Let it wash us wildly with its tongue
and shake its thick pelt. Let the dust rise off
in waves, in solar clouds, and let our old selves
float up in that haze, particles massed by the window,
motes among a thousand other motes. Now see
our two: we are the two motes laughing as they leave,
the two specks somersaulting right through the screen.

Let It Change

If you're anything like me, you have many days that are "born in sackcloth and ashes"—that is, days which at first feel difficult or downright impossible to bear. Yet a feeling or the mood of a moment can always shift toward delight or wonder, and often more completely than we might have expected. In "Let This Day," Annie Lighthart makes the case for not trying to force some immediate change in our outlook, and instead doing our best to give ourselves both time and space. "Let it change, rearrange," she says. I find much reassurance in this—in the way the day transforms into a wild dog, nudging its nose against the table "with joy." And how the past selves of the two people in the poem (no longer needed) turn into dust motes "laughing as they leave," tiny enough now to fly "right through the screen" of the open window.

Invitation for Writing and Reflection

Describe a time when you were able to sit back and stay with a difficult mood or emotion, until it changed into something else. And if you find yourself having one of those days right now, you might see how writing about your mind-state can also bring about a change in mood.

Laura Grace Weldon

COMMON GROUND

What's incomplete in me seeks refuge
in blackberry bramble and beech trees,
where creatures live without dogma
and water moves in patterns
more ancient than philosophy.
I stand still, child eavesdropping on her elders.
I don't speak the language
but my body translates as best it can,
wakening skin and gut, summoning
the long kinship we share with everything.

Rena Priest

TOUR OF A SALMONBERRY

A salmonberry is a
luminous spiral,
a golden basket,
woven of sunshine,
water, and birdsong.

I'm told that the birds
sing so sweet because
of all the berries they eat
and that is how you
can have a sweet voice too.

In my Native language,
the word for salmonberry
is *Alile'*. In Sanskrit, *Lila* means
'God plays.' Salmonberries
sometimes look that way.

Every year, they debut,
spectacular in the landscape,
worthy of their genus name:
Rubus spectabilis, meaning,
red sight worth seeing.

Each drupelet holds a seed
and the shimmering secret
kept by rain, of how to rise,
float above the earth, feel
the sun, and return.

Rosalie Sanara Petrouske

TRUE NORTH

In the woods, my father never needed a compass.
He told time by the sun's position.
When shadows grew long and slanted,
he still knew the way to turn
so we could find home.

We walked for miles, changed paths:
North, South, East, and West,
through golden tamaracks in autumn,
beneath old growth hemlocks, white pines,
and birches in summer.

If nightfall caught up to us, Father took my hand,
admonished me to watch for roots, burrows
tunneled into earth by badgers, woodchucks, or foxes.
At dusk, the Eastern screech owl's eerie trill
filled our ears as it swooped down from its perch
to devour a shrew or bat.

"If you think you are lost," Father told me, "travel downhill,
search for water, read the night sky," and he pointed
at Polaris perched at the tip of the Little Dipper's handle.

In daylight, he taught me why trees have more leaves on
    one side.
"To find true North," he said, "place a stick straight up in
    the ground,
mark where the stick's shadow lands with a rock."

But he was my true north, astride his shoulders
when I grew tired, I became taller than his six-foot frame.
His hands were the needle of my compass,
his voice my straight-edged arrow.

Connie Wanek

TALKING TO DAD

It's easier than picking up the phone,
whenever, wherever.
I need only the faintest signal
like a single thread of what used to be
his tennis shirt. Like an empty
chair at our table
into which a grandchild climbs.

After a bee leaves a clover blossom
the buzzing grows faint.
But there are many waves
in the infinite air,
and one of these carries an answer
to the simplest question.
He's fine, everything's fine.

Tyler Mortensen-Hayes

AFTER THE HEARTBREAK

It was summer, so of course the thrushes
were going berserk in the trees, singing
every song that came to them about
how astounding it is to be alive, to be breathing.
I was in the house, alone, my sobs echoing
through the empty rooms. The envelope
was sealed, the fire snubbed, the door
shut and locked. The end had come
and the world felt raw and harsh, like wind
on the inflamed skin that remains after
a sunburn is peeled away. *Don't*
touch me, I said to the wind, and to
the insistent waves of sun. *It's okay,*
I told my cowering little soul. *It's okay.*
Take what time you need. Retreat
to the downstairs room, draw the shades.
Some things, like just-planted seeds,
need isolation and dark. But I won't say
that something was planted. No,
instead, something was torn away—
many branches sliced from the trunk
of an old tree. And yet, something did,
eventually, emerge. What was it? All

I can tell you is that I'm here, writing
this—aren't I? And what would have happened
without the small tenderness I gave
to that wrecked thing I was? Don't the leaves
bloom anyway, on those branches
that are left? Don't they make themselves—
just by being alive, just by breathing—
beautiful again?

Ingrid Goff-Maidoff

THE LISTENING BRIDGE

Listen, heart, to the whispering of the World.
That is how it makes love to you.
—Rabindranath Tagore

When you come to the listening bridge,
you must be still there long enough
for the squirrels to sense you are of no harm;
for the birds to break their silence with singing
and the fluttering of wings; and for you,
and everything around you, to stop holding its breath.
And so, sit. Rest a while.
Give some wonder to the moss and purple violets.

Turn toward the sun and feel it warm your face.
Notice the rippling current of the spring-fed stream.
Allow a sense of softness to splash and filter in.
Trade the weight of all your seriousness
for the lightness of surrender—
by which I mean faith in a Presence
lovingly wiser than your self.
Remain quiet and listen
for what the voice born of stillness
might say: perhaps, simply:
Love. Carry on. Practice kindness.
Have affection for this day.

Brad Peacock

A MORNING IN THAILAND

Waking early, springing from bed
I pull on shorts, lace my running shoes, head out the door.
No thinking required, years of a morning routine,
thousands of miles spent in solitude.
I glide past yellow-robed monks praying in *wats*,
soaking up a culture of color,
listening to the gentle rhythm of motion.
They come out of nowhere,
this group of children laughing and smiling
with such play in their hearts
running beside me,
no language needed
just the sound of their joy, step for step.
I feel my heart unblocking
as dormant tears stream down my face,
their lesson as clear as their aura of innocence,
each one teaching me
how to love the world again.

Julia Fehrenbacher

THE ONLY WAY I KNOW TO LOVE THE WORLD

It is not just a cup of coffee
but the warm hum of hello, an invitation
to wake, to sip, to say *thank you*
for another chance to dance
with another new day.

It's not just a ceramic mug, but the one she
shaped with her own 16-year-old
hands, for me. For *me*.

It is not just one heart held open
to another, or a kiss blown in the mirror,
not just the soft circle of smile,
but a nod of—*I see you. You are not alone.*

Not just life. But *your* life. Your very temporary life.

It isn't just the earth you stand on
but the giver of every single thing, a reason
to get down on humbled, human knees
and say thank you thank you thank you.

It is not just another moment but a door flung open,
a flooded-with-light entrance to every real thing

not just a poem but a prayer whispered
from one listening ear
to another. The only way I know
to love the world.

Jacqueline Suskin

HOW TO FALL IN LOVE WITH YOURSELF

Sit in front of two candles,
one for each eye.
Light them and watch how the fire
takes its time with the wicks, nearly dying,
touching wax and climbing back into air
with a wave of hot yes.
Now, breathe each flame into the crown
of your head. There is a hole there
where elements can enter.
Your skull is a cup hungry for light.
Close your eyes and let
this glowing gift travel throughout
your entire body, take it down
slowly, like a dose of brilliant honey.
See how you overflow?
See how you do magic?
The warmth is red. It's white, orange,
blue and green. It touches every
part of you and when
the tailbone starts snaking,
when you become a tree,
you will love yourself completely
for burning with such ease.

Brad Aaron Modlin

ONE CANDLE NOW, THEN SEVEN MORE

I grew up in a family that did not tell
the story. I am listening to it now:

Even the morning you see a robin
flattened on the street, you hear

another in a tree, the notes
they've taught each other, bird

before bird before we were born.
And elsewhere, the rusty bicycle

carries the doctor all the way
across an island. He arrives in time.

Somewhere his sister adds water
to the soup until payday. And

over the final hill in a Southwestern
desert, a gas station appears. No,

the grief has not forgotten my name,
but this morning I tied

my shoelaces. Outside I can force
a wave at every face who might

need it. We might
spin till we collapse, but we still

have a hub: Even at dusk,
the sun isn't going anywhere.

We have lamps. The story insists
it just *looks* like there's only

enough oil to last one night.

Judith Chalmer

POCKET

Night time. It's quiet.
You're starting to shut down—
a yawn, an empty cup

carried to the sink. Nothing
complex—just a little need
for air. Anyway,

you're out the door.
Did I say February?
It's taken some time

to bundle up. The little park
is white under the lamp—
no one lingers, nor do you.

You walk, you turn home.
Breath, a still cloud.
No matter. A few months

and you'll hear some things
moving. You'll smell
the greening. You have this

for now—the winter
wood and its great
absorbent heart,

the young beech,
its dead leaves tiger bright.
The glitter above, the softness

below. Now you've come
to it. You reach down
in your pocket, step up

to your door. Here
are your cares. Slip off
your coat and be received.

Adele Kenny

SURVIVOR

A jay on the fence preaches to a
squirrel. I watch the squirrel quiver,
the way squirrels do—its whole
body flickers. I'm not sure why this
reminds me of when I was five and

something died in our drain spout.
Feather or fur, I watched my father
dig it out, knowing (as a child knows)
how much life matters. I have seen how
easily autumn shakes the yellow leaves,

how winter razes the shoals of heaven.
I have felt love's thunder and moan, and
had my night on the wild river. I have
heard the cancer diagnosis with my name
in it. I know what mercy is and isn't.

Morning breaks from sparrows' wings
(life's breezy business), and I'm still here,
still in love with the sorrows, the joys—
days like this, measured by memory, the
ticking crickets, the pulse in my wrist.

Lois Lorimer

RESCUE DOG

You came to us
around the time I was healing.
That windy chemo Spring
when I pulled out my hair
in fistfuls and it flew away
to line the nests of birds.
Hope snapped in the air
like prayer flags.

As I was losing my hair
in came yours: dark, abundant
soft for petting,
velcroed to sofas and carpets.
Help mate. Canine healer. You,
the shaggy blackboard
we scrawled our wishes on.

Yvonne Zipter

SEEDS

I brush the dog in the yard, and the wind whips
white wisps of fur airborne like milkweed seeds.
I imagine them taking root and sprouting
tiny greyhounds, the long stems of their legs,
slender heads like whimsical orchid blossoms.

But milkweed seeds themselves are miracle enough
for me, the way the pods part like curtains on a stage,
all the little ballerinas in their white tutus, the little swan
maidens, come gliding out, luminous in the sun's spotlight.
Delicate dancers, twirling out of sight like promises.

Most wondrous of all, though, is globe milkweed, each
pod—the color of a green anole—a prickly orb, an alien
spaceship, a hoop skirt airing on a line. Ripe, the pods
turn the color of unbleached linen, open like lockets,
spill out the milky dreams of seeds.

David Mook

MILKWEED

White folds of silken down
sleep in pods of darkness
until an awakening yawn
exhales its feathered breath,

and each on a silent sigh
carries a lone dark seed
with its own white soul
quietly into the new life.

Bradford Tice

MILKWEED

I tell myself softly, *this is how love begins*—
the air alive with something inconceivable,
seeds of every imaginable possibility
floating across the wet grasses, under
the thin arms of ferns. It drifts like snow
or old ash, settling on the dust of the roadways
as you and I descend into thickets, flanked
by the fragrance of honeysuckle and white
primrose.

I recall how my grandmother imagined
these wanderers were living beings,
some tiny phylum yet to be classified as life.
She would say they reminded her of maidens
decked in white dresses, waltzing through air.
Even after I showed her the pods from which
they sprang, blossoming like tiny spiders,
she refused to believe.

Now, standing beside you in the crowded
autumn haze, I watch them flock, emerge from
brittle stalks, bursting upon the world as
young lovers do—trysting in the tall grasses,
resting fingers lightly in tousled hair.
Listen, and you can hear them whisper
in the rushes, gazing out at us, wondering—
what lives are these?

Jane Hirshfield

SOLSTICE

The Earth today tilts one way, then another.

And yes, though all things change,
this night again will watch its fireflies,
then go in to a bed with sheets,
to lights, a beloved.

To running water cold and hot.

Take nothing for granted,
you who were also opulent, a stung cosmos.

Birds sang, frogs sang, their *sufficient unto*.
The late-night rain-bringing thunder.

And if days grew ordinarily shorter,
the dark's mirror lengthened,

and one's gain was not the other lessened.

Julie Cadwallader Staub

REVERENCE

The air vibrated
with the sound of cicadas
on those hot Missouri nights after sundown
when the grown-ups gathered on the wide back lawn,
sank into their slung-back canvas chairs
tall glasses of iced tea beading in the heat

and we sisters chased fireflies
reaching for them in the dark
admiring their compact black bodies
their orange stripes and seeking antennas
as they crawled to our fingertips
and clicked open into the night air.

In all the days and years that have followed,
I don't know that I've ever experienced
that same utter certainty of the goodness of life
that was as palpable
as the sound of the cicadas on those nights:

my sisters running around with me in the dark,
the murmur of the grown-ups' voices,
the way reverence mixes with amazement
to see such a small body
emit so much light.

Jennifer G. Lai

IN MY MIND'S CORAL, MOTHER STILL CALLS US FROM INSIDE

that summer, we were little chemists, bakers,
storefront merchants hawking our wares. I had never
been to a night market before, but mother told me
they had everything you could ever want. for us,

there were slick mud pies, glossy from the cool shade,
blistering on the raw white concrete.   sunset-pink
petals from the Big House down the street. warm
daisy chains, holy dandelions, dry whispering grass.

back then, the boy next door was just   a boy next door.
whatever he said I forgot by morning. whenever we could play,
we played. whenever the leaves were plump, lucky, full
of milk—we collected them.

one day, a rare antidote for deadly poison
and another, a welcome cure for broken arms,
and then a lost currency
and sometimes new shampoo for my dolls.

what we knew then, was   there was nothing
that could hurt us   save for scraped knees,
or the fat green Japanese beetle
shimmer-zip buzzing past our ears.

we just rinsed off our dirty heels,
hosed off plastic sandals and that was good enough.
the wasps' nest in the rafters, broken,
too high up to see.

Worlds of Wonder

We often call it nostalgia when we look back with joy on those simpler, more innocent times in our lives. "In My Mind's Coral, Mother Still Calls Us from Inside" illustrates certain periods in life truly *are* less complicated—before our culture, families, and peers place their expectations and limitations on us, before a larger awareness of the world seeps in. Here, Jennifer G. Lai transports us back to a summer in childhood when she and her friends made their own worlds to inhabit and found the miraculous in small things like "daisy chains, holy dandelions, dry whispering grass." By the end of the poem, we understand that "the wasps' nest in the rafters" might symbolize all the difficult knowledge that remains too far off, "too high up to see" for now. By admitting us into her private, long-ago world, where the worst worries were "scraped knees, or the fat green Japanese beetle shimmer-zip buzzing past our ears," the speaker reminds us of the wonders that might still be possible, if only we could reclaim that freer, more expansive way of being in our child selves.

Invitation for Writing and Reflection

Can you remember a time from childhood when the world was a place of safety and wonder? Describe some of the private rituals and delights from that time. You might try beginning with Lai's phrase "That summer, we were . . ." and see where it leads you.

Rosemerry Wahtola Trommer

LATENT

Riding our bikes through the warm summer night,
the dark itself parted to let us pass;
wind in our hair, soft whir of the wheels—
and an almost irrational joy grew in me then,
such simple joy, as if joy were always here,
waiting to flourish, needing only to be noticed.

And is joy latent in everything?
I have felt it sometimes in the washing
of dishes, in mowing the lawn,
in peeling the carrots, even washing
the fishtank and scrubbing the floor.

So could it be, too, inside worried pacing?
In envy? In sighing? In the clenching of fists?
Is there joy where I can't imagine it?
Joy—waiting to spin like a wheel,
waiting to rise like laughter
that careens through the deepening dark.

Charles Rossiter

TRANSFORMATION

every heart is its own Buddha
to become a saint, do nothing.
—Shih Shu

The day is warm and cloudless,
the lake a trembling blue

kayakers glide by
seemingly without effort

a light breeze, soft,
like angel's breath.

I read and write, relaxed,
while ever so slowly

like a miracle you can
actually watch happen,

without even trying,
my skin is turning brown.

Tony Hoagland

FIELD GUIDE

Once, in the cool blue middle of a lake,
up to my neck in that most precious element of all,

I found a pale-gray, curled-upwards pigeon feather
floating on the tension of the water

at the very instant when a dragonfly,
like a blue-green iridescent bobby pin,

hovered over it, then lit, and rested.
That's all.

I mention this in the same way
that I fold the corner of a page

in certain library books,
so that the next reader will know

where to look for the good parts.

Rage Hezekiah

LAKE SUNAPEE

for Jess

I rise to find
your face

awash in steam
dark coffee

cupped between
calloused hands

the morning
bathed in sunlight

aspens cloaked
in fresh snow

you look up
from your book

eyes dark-rimmed
jungle cat

thirst-slaked
when we first kissed

years ago
on a dance floor

dimly-lit with
greenish light

I thought you
wore mascara

now I know
your hunger

natural kohl
black lashes

there before & after
you wake

home is where
the kettle whistles

midday we return
from local woods

I watch you
pull a ribbon

of honey into
handmade mugs

sweeten two
cups of tea

we sit quietly
at ease

love
know this

you are who
I asked for

on my knees

HOW TO LOVE

After stepping into the world again,
there is that question of how to love,
how to bundle yourself against the frosted morning—
the crunch of icy grass underfoot, the scrape
of cold wipers along the windshield—
and convert time into distance.

What song to sing down an empty road
as you begin your morning commute?
And is there enough in you to see, really see,
the three wild turkeys crossing the street
with their featherless heads and stilt-like legs
in search of a morning meal? Nothing to do
but hunker down, wait for them to safely cross.

As they amble away, you wonder if they want
to be startled back into this world. Maybe you do, too,
waiting for all this to give way to love itself,
to look into the eyes of another and feel something—
the pleasure of a new lover in the unbroken night,
your wings folded around him, on the other side
of this ragged January, as if a long sleep has ended.

READING GROUP QUESTIONS AND TOPICS FOR DISCUSSION

"The Grove" by Michael Kleber-Diggs (page 17)

- Michael Kleber-Diggs speaks from the point of view of a grove of trees. How might he also be speaking for all of humanity here? How might we "make vast shelter together" by recognizing how interconnected we all are?

- As this poem indicates, there are many different types of trees, yet the poet says we are "the same the same, not different." How might we make it a practice to turn our wonder toward all the ways we're similar as humans, rather than how we're separate?

INVITATION FOR WRITING AND REFLECTION

- Find a grove of trees and stand or sit among them for as long as you can. Describe what sensory impressions come to you, whether they feel factually true or not.

"Lately" by Laure-Anne Bosselaar (page 22)

- Begin by answering the questions that come in the final lines of this poem. Do you believe that moments sometimes return to us so they might come alive again in the retelling? How do your own moments come back to you?

- Describe a recent time when something seemed to reach for your attention. How did it feel to be called to like that, to notice something out of the blue? Consider the "luck" that Bosselaar mentions in the poem. Why do you think we find such delight in the simple things of nature?

INVITATION FOR WRITING AND REFLECTION

- See if you can re-create a similar moment of "luck" that you experienced when a sense of awe or wonder called you back to the physical world around you.

"Stopped Again by the Sea" by Mark Nepo
(page 42)

- Mark Nepo describes a moment of deep peace he felt while sailing in childhood. What does his description of this memory bring up for you? Why do you think we often find the water of rivers, creeks, lakes, and oceans so calming? What "unseen force" seems to speak to us when we're near water?

- Do you agree with the speaker's description of love at the end of the poem, how by revealing all that we hide, we move beyond our own hidden secrets?

INVITATION FOR WRITING AND REFLECTION

- Keeping in mind the strong images of this poem, what scenes or memories of your own conjure a sense of peace for you? Was there some ritual in childhood that allowed you to escape briefly from the noise of the world?

"To Hold" by Li-Young Lee (page 50)

- This poem begins with the startling statement "So we're dust." What you do think Lee means by this, and why would he start a love poem this way? Lee also says that fear has often led him "to abandon what I know I must relinquish." How does he stay with those difficult feelings in this instance?

- How does this fear show up in your own life, especially with loved ones? Are there ways we might keep it from disrupting the peace we feel in the "joint and fragile keeping" we create together?

INVITATION FOR WRITING AND REFLECTION

- Describe a time when you were able to hold on to a feeling of connection even when you were anxious that you might lose the other person. What allowed you to stay in the wonder of that moment?

"Joint Custody" by Ada Limón (page 53)

- How does Limón immediately reframe the difficulty of her parents' divorce when she was a child? Though she now wishes she could have recognized the "abundance" and wonder of having two families, how does Limón also own the sorrow and challenge of that time?
- Toward the end, she says she now has "Two entirely different brains." What might be the benefits of this, being able to hold both joy and sorrow in the very same instance?

INVITATION FOR WRITING AND REFLECTION

- Write about a difficulty that you've been able to reframe and see differently over time. How has your view of this challenge changed over the years, and why do you see it now in a more positive light?

"Chestnut" by Rebecca Baggett (page 59)

- The speaker acknowledges the distressing disappearance of chestnut trees in the United States yet chooses to focus more on the wonder of having touched "a young chestnut." Why is this scene of rebirth so important? Though she acknowledges her own grief in this poem, how does the speaker also point to the potentially positive aspect of loss?
- Have you ever felt a sense of renewal after grief or tragedy, the "rising" and transformation that Baggett finds in this sapling?

INVITATION FOR WRITING AND REFLECTION

- As you look around, see if you can find small examples, especially in nature, of resilience and renewal that remind us how loss "may shelter some new thing" within us.

"Amends" by Jessica Gigot (page 82)

- Why does the speaker feel such "muddied pride" in holding her "homegrown head of broccoli"? What does it mean to make "amends with the earth," as Gigot describes here. Given the title of the poem, why is the word "amends" so important?

- Toward the end, the speaker says of her homegrown vegetable, "Sweat makes this one something special." How can regular attention and care transform our relationship to the earth, other people, and even ourselves over time?

INVITATION FOR WRITING AND REFLECTION
- Recall a moment when you took pride in something that you had grown or made yourself. Write with a sense of marvel and amazement at your own creation. Did it have any healing effects on you?

"My Mother's Colander" by Dorianne Laux
(page 85)
- What do we learn about the speaker of this poem simply from her descriptions of the old colander once belonging to her mother? Which details stand out to you? Have you ever felt a deep connection to some everyday object that belonged to another person? Why do you think we hold onto the possessions of loved ones, long after they're gone?
- Think about all the ways this colander transforms as the poet's descriptions unfold. What memories or objects from the past does this poem call forth for you?

INVITATION FOR WRITING AND REFLECTION
- Choose some object you have kept over the years that's now become beautiful with use. Describe it in vivid detail as Dorianne Laux does here, letting the images tell the story of this well-loved thing.

"Your Soft Heart" by Nikita Gill (page 109)
- Consider the power of repetition in this poem. Why would the poet choose to use the words "You are still" over and over? Why do we sometimes lose that sense of a "soft heart," armoring up instead of letting ourselves feel empathy for plants and animals, and grief for other people suffering elsewhere in the world?

- How might we bring ourselves back to the wonder that allows us to care for the small things around us, remembering that, although kindness feels "endangered," we are each still "so full with it"?

INVITATION FOR WRITING AND REFLECTION
- What are some of the ways your own "soft heart" showed up in childhood, in the ways that you once cared for the world? How does this essential kindness still guide you in the ways that you cultivate peace and healing for those around you?

"Latent" by Rosemerry Wahtola Trommer (page 166)

- A simple burst of joy felt while riding bikes with a loved one leads the speaker to the question "And is joy latent in everything?" Do you believe that joy always lives inside us, "waiting to flourish"? She also confesses that she has found joy in chores like washing the dishes or mowing the lawn. Have there been times when you felt surprised by a sudden and "irrational joy"? How did you feel it in your body?
- At the end, the speaker takes the question further, wondering if joy might live in "worried pacing" and "envy," "where I can't imagine it." How might we stretch our own definitions of joy so that the word includes every deep feeling that renews us and reminds us we are alive?

INVITATION FOR WRITING AND REFLECTION
- Tell the story of a time when you were doing something ordinary yet felt a burst of joy rising "like laughter" in you. You might also list other times when you felt the renewal of joy while doing some plain and simple task that somehow led you to a new place.

POET BIOGRAPHIES

José A. Alcántara lives in western Colorado. He is the author of *The Bitten World* (Tebot Bach). He has worked as a bookseller, mailman, electrician, commercial fisherman, baker, carpenter, studio photographer, door-to-door salesman, and math teacher. His poems have appeared in *Poetry Daily*, American Life in Poetry, *The Slowdown*, *Ploughshares*, *32 Poems*, the *Southern Review*, and the anthologies *The Path to Kindness: Poems of Connection and Joy* and *America, We Call Your Name: Poems of Resistance and Resilience*. (p. 96)

Lahab Assef Al-Jundi's poetry has appeared in collections such as *In These Latitudes: Ten Contemporary Poets* and *Inclined to Speak: An Anthology of Arab American Poetry*, as well as many other anthologies and literary journals. His most recent poetry collections are *No Faith at All* (Pecan Grove Press) and *This Is It* (Kelsay Books). (p. 83)

Born in New York City in 1950, **Julia Alvarez** has written ten novels, including *How the García Girls Lost Their Accents*, *In the Time of the Butterflies*, and *Afterlife*, as well as poetry collections, including *Homecoming*, *The Other Side/El Otro Lado*, and *The Woman I Kept to Myself*. Alvarez's awards include the Pura Belpré and Américas Awards for her books for young readers, the Hispanic Heritage Award, and the F. Scott Fitzgerald Award. In 2013, she received the National Medal of Arts from President Obama. (p. 20)

James Armstrong is the author of *Monument in a Summer Hat* (New Issues Press) and *Blue Lash* (Milkweed Editions), and coauthor of *Nature, Culture and Two Friends Talking* (North Star Press). He teaches English at Winona State University in Winona, Minnesota, where he was the city's first poet laureate. He is the cofounder of the Maria W. Faust Sonnet Contest, an international poetry competition. (p. 12)

Zeina Azzam is a Palestinian American poet, editor, and community activist. Her chapbook, *Bayna Bayna: In-Between,* was released in 2021 by The Poetry Box. Zeina's poems are published or are forthcoming in *Pleiades, Passager, Gyroscope, Pensive Journal, Streetlight Magazine, Mizna, Sukoon Magazine, Barzakh, Making Levantine Cuisine, Tales from Six Feet Apart, Bettering American Poetry, Making Mirrors: Writing/Righting by and for Refugees, Gaza Unsilenced,* and others. She holds an MA in Arabic literature from Georgetown University. (p. 60)

Rebecca Baggett is the author of four chapbook collections and *The Woman Who Lives Without Money* (Regal House Publishing), winner of the Terry J. Cox Award. A native of North Carolina, she has lived most of her adult life in Athens, Georgia, where she worked as an academic advisor at UGA. In retirement, she stewards a Little Free Library, gardens, dreams of travel, and chases the two-year-old grandson who reconciles her to staying home. (p. 59)

Nina Bagley is a jewelry designer, mixed media artist, and writer living a quiet life in a small log cabin out in the rural woods of western North Carolina. Inspiration for her work comes from the natural world that surrounds her; creating art with natural findings brings a sweet pleasure, as does hammering words of longing for natural connections into silver or scrawling them across old scraps of weathered paper. (p. 122)

Wendell Berry is a poet, novelist, essayist, environmental activist, and farmer. He is the author of more than fifty books of various genres and has farmed the same ancestral land in Port Royal, Kentucky, for the past forty years. Berry's poetry collections include *This Day: Collected & New Sabbath Poems, Given,* and *A Timbered Choir: The Sabbath Poems 1979–1997.* (p. 5)

George Bilgere's seventh book of poems, *Blood Pages,* came out from the University of Pittsburgh Press in 2018. His other collections include

Imperial, The White Museum, Haywire, The Good Kiss, Big Bang, and *The Going.* He has received the Midland Authors Prize, the May Swenson Poetry Award, a Pushcart Prize, a grant from the National Endowment for the Arts, a Fulbright Fellowship, a Witter Bynner Fellowship, and the Cleveland Arts Prize. He teaches at John Carroll University in Cleveland, Ohio, where he lives with his wife and two exceptionally fine boys. (p. 46)

Kimberly Blaeser, past Wisconsin poet laureate and founding director of In-Na-Po, Indigenous Nations Poets, is the author of five poetry collections, including *Copper Yearning, Apprenticed to Justice,* and *Résister en dansant/Ikwe-niimi: Dancing Resistance.* An enrolled member of the White Earth Nation, Blaeser is an Anishinaabe activist and environmentalist, a professor emerita at University of Wisconsin–Milwaukee, and an MFA faculty member at the Institute of American Indian Arts in Santa Fe. kblaeser.org (p. 64)

Sally Bliumis-Dunn's poems have appeared in *On the Seawall, Paris Review, Prairie Schooner, PLUME, Poetry London,* the *New York Times,* PBS NewsHour, *upstreet,* Poem-a-day, and Ted Kooser's column, among others. In 2018, her third book, *Echolocation* (Plume Editions/MadHat Press) was longlisted for the Julie Suk Award, runner-up for the Eric Hoffer Prize, and runner-up for the Poetry by the Sea Prize. (p. 119)

Laure-Anne Bosselaar is the author of *The Hour Between Dog and Wolf, Small Gods of Grief* (Isabella Gardner Prize for Poetry), *A New Hunger* (ALA Notable Book), and *These Many Rooms.* A Pushcart Prize recipient, she edited five anthologies. She taught at Sarah Lawrence College and University of California–Santa Barbara. The winner of the 2020 James Dickey Poetry Prize, she served as Santa Barbara's poet laureate (2019–2021). (p. 22)

An enrolled member of the Nulhegan Abenaki nation, **Joseph Bruchac's** work often reflects his Indigenous ancestry and the Adirondack region of New York State where he was raised by his grandparents and has lived throughout his life. The author of over 170 books in many different genres, he's also a traditional Native musician and storyteller. His most recent book, *A Year of Moons*, personal essays about his life and the life around him in the Adirondack foothills, was published by Fulcrum Books. (pp. 14, 107)

Paola Bruni is a two-time Pushcart Prize nominee and a winner of the Morton Marcus Poetry Prize and the Muriel Craft Bailey Poetry Prize, as well as a finalist for the Mudfish Poetry Prize. Her poems have appeared in the *Southern Review*, *Ploughshares*, *Five Points Journal*, *Rattle*, *Massachusetts Review*, *Comstock Review*, and elsewhere. Her debut book of poetry is an epistolary collection titled *How Do You Spell the Sound of Crickets* (Paper Angel Press). (p. 88)

Carolyn Chilton Casas lives on the central coast of California, where she loves hiking and playing beach volleyball. She is a Reiki master and teacher, and often explores ways of healing in her writing. Carolyn's work has appeared in *Braided Way*, *Energy Magazine*, A Network for Grateful Living, *Reiki News Magazine*, and *Touch Magazine*. You can read more of her work online and in her first collection of poems, *Our Shared Breath*. (p. 43)

Judith Chalmer is the author of *Minnow* (Kelsay Books) and *Out of History's Junk Jar* (Time Being Books). She is cotranslator of two books of haiku and tanka with Michiko Oishi, *Red Fish Alphabet* (Honami Syoten) and *Deepening Snow* (Plowboy Press). In 2018, she received the Arthur Williams Award from the Vermont Arts Council for Meritorious Service in the Arts. She lives with her partner, Lisa, in Vermont. (p. 155)

Patricia Clark is the author of six volumes of poetry, including *Sunday Rising*, *The Canopy*, and most recently *Self Portrait with a Million Dollars*. Her work has appeared in *The Atlantic*, *Gettysburg Review*, *Poetry*, and *Slate*, among others. Patricia's awards include a Creative Artist Grant in Michigan, the Mississippi Review Prize, the Gwendolyn Brooks Prize, and cowinner of the Lucille Medwick Prize from the Poetry Society of America. She also received the 2018 Book of the Year Award from the Poetry Society of Virginia for *The Canopy*. (p. 126)

Kai Coggin (she/her) is the author of four collections, most recently *Mining for Stardust* (FlowerSong Press). She is a teaching artist in poetry with the Arkansas Arts Council and the host of the longest-running consec-utive weekly open mic series in the country, Wednesday Night Poetry. Her widely pub-lished poems have appeared in Poetry, *Prairie Schooner*, *SWWIM*, *Lavender Review*, and elsewhere. She lives

with her wife in Hot Springs National Park, Arkansas. (p. 25)

Sharon Corcoran lives in southern Colorado. She translated (from French) the writings of North African explorer Isabelle Eberhardt in the works *In the Shadow of Islam* and *Prisoner of Dunes*, published by Peter Owen Ltd., London. Her poems have appeared in *Braided Way*, *Canary*, *Buddhist Poetry Review*, *One Art*, *Sisyphus*, *Literary North*, and *Bearings Online*, among other journals. She is the author of two books of poetry, *Inventory* (KDP) and *The Two Worlds* (Middle Creek). (p. 95)

James Crews is the editor of several anthologies, including *The Path to Kindness: Poems of Connection and Joy* and the best-selling *How to Love the World*, which has been featured on NPR's *Morning Edition*, in the *Boston Globe*, and in the *Washington Post*. He is the author of four prize-winning collections of poetry: *The Book of What Stays*, *Telling My Father*, *Bluebird*, and *Every Waking Moment*. He lives with his husband in Southern Vermont. jamescrews.net (pp. 9, 35, 76)

Barbara Crooker is the author of nine books of poetry; *Some Glad Morning* (University of Pittsburgh Press) is the latest. Her honors include the W. B. Yeats Society of New York Award, the Thomas Merton Poetry of the Sacred Award, and three Pennsylvania Council on the Arts Fellowships. Her work appears in a variety of literary journals and anthologies and has been read on ABC, the BBC, and The Writer's Almanac and featured on Ted Kooser's American Life in Poetry. (p. 115)

An Officer of the Order of Canada, **Lorna Crozier** has been acknowledged for her contributions to Canadian literature with five honorary doctorates, most recently from McGill and Simon Fraser Universities. Her books have received numerous national awards, including the Governor-General's Award for Poetry. A professor emerita at the University of Victoria, she has performed for Queen Elizabeth II and has read her poetry, which has been translated into several languages, on every continent except Antarctica. She lives on Vancouver Island. (p. 33)

Toi Derricotte was the recipient of the Academy of American Poets' 2021 Wallace Stevens Award and the Poetry Society of America's 2020 Frost Medal for distinguished lifetime achievement in poetry. She is the author of National Book Awards Finalist *I: New & Selected Poems*, *The Undertaker's Daughter*, and four earlier collections of poetry, including *Tender*, winner of the Paterson Poetry Prize. Her literary memoir, *The Black Notebooks*, was a *New York Times* Notable Book of the Year. (p. 18)

Rita Dove published her first book of poems, *The Yellow House on the Corner*, in 1980. She has followed this work with several other collections, including *Museum*, *Thomas and Beulah*, *Grace Notes*, *Selected Poems*, *Mother Love*, *On the Bus with Rosa Parks*, and *American Smooth*. In 1993, Dove became poet laureate of the United States, the first Black poet to receive this honor. (p. 16)

Meghan Dunn is the author of *Curriculum*, winner of the 2020 Barry Spacks Poetry Prize from Gunpowder Press. She lives in Brooklyn, where she teaches high school English. Her work has appeared in *Narrative*, *Poetry Northwest*, and *Four Way Review* and has been featured on *Verse Daily* and *The Slowdown* podcast. She is a recipient of scholarships from the Bread Loaf Writers' Conference and the Sewanee Writers' Conference. (p. 72)

Joanne Durham is the author of *To Drink from a Wider Bowl* (Evening Street Press), winner of the Sinclair Poetry Prize, and *On Shifting Shoals* (Kelsay Books). A retired educator, she lives on the North Carolina coast, with the ocean as her backyard and muse. When not writing poetry, she practices yoga, delights in her grandkids, and works for a better world for them to grow up in. joannedurham.com (p. 71)

Peg Edera is a native of Portland, Maine. She migrated to Portland, Oregon, 35 years ago. She writes in community most days of the week. She is the author of a collection of poetry, *Love Is Deeper Than Distance: Poems of love, death, a little sex, ALS, dementia, and the widow's life thereafter* (Fernwood Press). Her work has also appeared in *Friends Journal, Untold Volumes: Feminist Theology Poetry,* and the OPA anthology *Pandemic,* among others. (p. 56)

Terri Kirby Erickson is the author of six collections, including *A Sun Inside My Chest* (Press 53). Her work has appeared in American Life in Poetry, *Atlanta Review, Healing the Divide: Poems of Kindness and Connection, How to Love the World: Poems of Gratitude and Hope, Christian Century, The Sun,* The Writer's Almanac, and many others. Her awards include the Joy Harjo Poetry Prize, the Atlanta Review International Publication Prize, and a Nautilus Silver Book Award. She lives in North Carolina. (p. 134)

Anne Evans was born and raised on California's central coast. After leaving a long career in secondary education, she joined an AWA group, and her writing practice became more intentional and consistent. During the pandemic, she wrote a poem every day and recently self-published 80 of those poems in a collection called *Peace in the Pandemic*. She continues this healing and enriching daily writing routine, living in Northern California with her husband and her dog, close to her kids and grandkids. (p. 114)

Joseph Fasano is a poet, novelist, and songwriter. His novels include *The Swallows of Lunetto* (Maudlin House) and *The Dark Heart of Every Wild Thing* (Platypus Press). His books of poetry include *The Crossing*, *Vincent*, *Inheritance*, and *Fugue for Other Hands*. His honors include the Cider Press Review Book Award, the Rattle Poetry Prize, seven Pushcart Prize nominations, and a nomination for the Poets' Prize. His debut album, *The Wind That Knows the Way*, is available wherever music is sold or streamed. (p. 129)

Julia Fehrenbacher is a poet, a teacher, a life coach, and a sometimes-painter who is always looking for ways to spread a little good around in this world. She is most at home by the ocean and in the forests of the Pacific Northwest and with pen and paintbrush in hand. She lives in Corvallis, Oregon, with her husband and two beautiful girls. (p. 151)

Laura Foley is the author of seven poetry collections. *Why I Never Finished My Dissertation* received a starred *Kirkus* review and an Eric Hoffer Award. Her collection *It's This* is forthcoming from Fernwood Press. Her poems have won numerous awards and national recognition, been read by Garrison Keillor on The Writer's Almanac, and appeared in Ted Kooser's American Life in Poetry. Laura lives with her wife, Clara Gimenez, among Vermont hills. (pp. 91, 104)

Rudy Francisco is one of the most recognizable names in Spoken Word Poetry. He was born, was raised, and still resides in San Diego, California. As an artist, Rudy Francisco is an amalgamation of social critique, introspection, honesty, and humor. He uses personal narratives to discuss the politics of race, class, gender, and religion while simultaneously pinpointing and reinforcing the interconnected nature of human existence. He is the author of *I'll Fly Away* (Button Poetry). (p. 47)

Albert Garcia is the author of three books of poems, *Rainshadow* (Copper Beech Press), *Skunk Talk* (Bear Star Press), and *A Meal Like That* (Brick Road Poetry Press), as well as a textbook called *Digging In: Literature for Developing Writers* (Prentice Hall). His poems have appeared in journals such as *Prairie Schooner, Willow Springs, Southern Poetry Review*, and *North American Review*. He has worked most of his career at Sacramento City College both as professor and administrator. (p. 10)

Ross Gay is the author of four books of poetry: *Against Which*; *Bringing the Shovel Down*; *Catalog of Unabashed Gratitude*, winner of the 2015 National Book Critics Circle Award and the 2016 Kingsley Tufts Poetry Award; and *Be Holding* (University of Pittsburgh Press). His best-selling collection of essays, *The Book of Delights*, was released by Algonquin Books, and he is the author most recently of *Inciting Joy* (Algonquin). (p. 27)

Jessica Gigot is a poet, farmer, and coach. She lives on a little sheep farm in the Skagit Valley. Her second book of poems, *Feeding Hour* (Wandering Aengus Press), won a Nautilus Award and was a finalist for the 2021 Washington State Book Award. Jessica's writing and reviews appear in *Orion*, the *New York Times*, the *Seattle Times, Ecotone, Terrain.org, Gastronomica, Crab Creek Review*, and *Poetry Northwest*. Her memoir, *A Little Bit of Land*, was published by Oregon State University Press in 2022. (p. 82)

Nikita Gill is a British-Indian poet, playwright, writer, and illustrator based in the south of England. Gill's work was first published when she was 12 years old, and she has since published eight volumes of poetry, including *Your Soul Is a River*; *Wild Embers: Poems of Rebellion, Fire, and Beauty*; *Fierce Fairytales: Poems & Stories to Stir Your Soul*; *Great Goddesses: Life Lessons from Myths and Monsters*; *Your Heart Is the Sea*; *The Girl and the Goddess*; *Where Hope Comes From: Poems of Resilience, Healing, and Light*; and *These Are the Words: Fearless Verse to Find Your Voice*. (pp. 24, 109)

Sue Ann Gleason grew up in the arms of an Italian American immigrant family who shaped her young mind and gave her perspectives and memories that you will see sprinkled throughout her poetry. She is a writer, a teacher, and an activist. Sue Ann holds inspired writing circles and organizes grassroots efforts, nurturing both individuals and agents for change in an increasingly complex world. Her book *in the glint of broken glass* can be found at wellnourishedwoman.com. (p. 86)

Ingrid Goff-Maidoff is the author of more than a dozen books of poetry and inspiration, as well as the creator of a line of cards and gifts. Her books include *What Holds Us*, *Wild Song*, *Befriending the Soul*, *Good Mother Welcome*, and *Simple Graces for Every Meal*. She lives on Martha's Vineyard with her husband and three white cats: Rumi, Hafiz, and Mirabai. Ingrid celebrates poetry, beauty & spirit through her website: tendingjoy.com. (p. 149)

Natalie Goldberg is the author of fourteen books, including *Writing Down the Bones*, which has sold over a million-and-a-half copies and been translated into fourteen languages. Her latest book is *Three Simple Lines: A Writer's Pilgrimage into the Heart and Homeland of Haiku*. Goldberg has been teaching seminars in writing as a practice for the last thirty years. Her lively paintings can be viewed at the Ernesto Mayans Gallery on Canyon Road in

Santa Fe. She currently lives in northern New Mexico. nataliegoldberg.com (p. 58)

Leah Naomi Green is the author of *The More Extravagant Feast* (Graywolf Press), selected by Li-Young Lee for the Walt Whitman Award of the Academy of American Poets. She is the recipient of a 2021 Treehouse Climate Action Poetry Prize, as well as the 2021 Lucille Clifton Legacy Award. Green teaches environmental studies and English at Washington and Lee University. She lives in the mountains of Virginia, where she and her family homestead and grow food. (p. 80)

Lucy Griffith lives beside the Guadalupe River near Comfort, Texas. As a retired psychologist, she explored the imagined life of the Burro Lady of West Texas in her debut collection, *We Make a Tiny Herd*, earning both the Wrangler and Willa Prizes. Her second collection, *Wingbeat Atlas*, pairs her poems with images by wildlife photographer Ken Butler, to celebrate our citizens of the sky. The collection

was released in May 2022 by FlowerSong Press. She has been a Bread Loaf scholar, is a Certified Master Naturalist, and is always happiest on a tractor named Mabel. (p. 54)

Joy Harjo served as the 23rd US poet laureate, the first Native American to hold the position, and the only poet to be awarded a third term. Born in Tulsa, Oklahoma, Harjo is an internationally renowned performer and writer of the Muscogee (Creek) Nation. She is the author of nine books of poetry, several plays and children's books, and two memoirs. (p. 92)

Penny Harter's collection of haibun, *Keeping Time: Haibun for the Journey*, is forthcoming from Kelsay Books, joining her recent collections *Still-Water Days* and *A Prayer the Body Makes*. Her work appears in *Persimmon Tree*, *Rattle*, *Tiferet*, and American Life in Poetry, and in many journals, anthologies, and earlier collections. She has won fellowships and awards from the Dodge Foundation, the New Jersey State Council on the Arts, the Poetry Society of America, and the Virginia Center for Creative Arts. pennyharterpoet.com (p. 130)

Margaret Hasse lives in Saint Paul, Minnesota, where she has been active as a teaching poet, among other work in the community. Six of Margaret's full-length poetry collections are in print. During the first year of the COVID-19 pandemic, Margaret collaborated with artist Sharon DeMark on *Shelter*, a collection of poems and paintings about refuge. A chapbook, *The Call of Glacier Park*, is her latest publication. MargaretHasse.com (p. 98)

Rage Hezekiah is a New England–based poet and educator who earned her MFA from Emerson College. She has received fellowships from Cave Canem, MacDowell, and the Ragdale Foundation, and is a recipient of the Saint Botolph Foundation's Emerging Artists Award. Her poems have been anthologized, cotranslated, and published internationally, and her most recent book is *Yearn* (Diode Editions). (pp. 84, 169)

Donna Hilbert's latest book is *Gravity: New & Selected Poems* (Tebot Bach). Her new collection, *Threnody*, is forthcoming from Moon Tide Press. She is a monthly contributing writer to the online journal *Verse-Virtual*. Her work has appeared in the *Los Angeles Times, Braided Way, Chiron Review, Sheila-Na-Gig, Rattle, Zocalo Public Square, One Art*, and numerous anthologies. She writes and leads private workshops in Southern California, where she makes her home. donnahilbert.com (p. 52)

AE Hines grew up in rural North Carolina and now divides his time between Charlotte and Medellín, Colombia. His first poetry collection, *Any Dumb Animal*, was released in 2021, and his work has also appeared in *Southern Review, Poet Lore, Alaska Quarterly Review, Ninth Letter, Greensboro Review, Missouri Review, RHINO Poetry*, and *I-70 Review*, among other places. aehines.net (p. 40)

Jane Hirshfield's ninth, recently published poetry collection is *Ledger* (Knopf). Her work appears in the *New Yorker, The Atlantic*, the

Times Literary Supplement, the *New York Review of Books,* and ten editions of The Best American Poetry. A former chancellor of the Academy of American Poets, she was elected to the American Academy of Arts & Sciences in 2019. (p. 162)

Tony Hoagland (1953–2018) was the author of numerous poetry collections, including *Sweet Ruin*; *Donkey Gospel*, winner of the James Laughlin Award; *What Narcissism Means to Me*, a finalist for the National Book Critics Circle Award; *Rain*; and *Unincorporated Persons in the Late Honda Dynasty*. He also published two collections of essays about poetry: *Real Sofistakashun* and *Twenty Poems That Could Save America and Other Essays.* (p. 168)

Linda Hogan is a Chickasaw poet, novelist, essayist, playwright, teacher, and activist who has spent most of her life in Oklahoma and Colorado. Her fiction has garnered many honors, including a Pulitzer Prize nomination, and her poetry collections have received an American Book Award, a Colorado Book Award, and a National Book Critics Circle nomination. Her latest book is *A History of Kindness* (Torrey House Press). (p. 61)

Mary Jo LoBello Jerome is the author of *Torch the Empty Fields* (Finishing Line Press). Her work has appeared in *Paterson Literary Review, Poets Reading the News, Literary North, River Heron Review, Little Patuxent Review,* and the *New York Times,* among others. A poetry editor of Schuylkill Valley Journal and the 2019 poet laureate of Bucks County, Pennsylvania, she led the editing committee of *Fire Up the Poems,* a poetry guidebook for teachers. (p. 79)

Jacqueline Jules is the author of *Manna in the Morning* (Kelsay Books) and *Itzhak Perlman's Broken String,* winner of the 2016 Helen Kay Chapbook Prize from Evening Street Press. Her poetry has appeared in over 100 publications, including the *Sunlight Press, Gyroscope Review,* and *One Art.* She is also the author of a collection for young readers, *Tag Your Dreams:*

Poems of Play and Persistence (Albert Whitman). jacquelinejules.com (p. 38)

Adele Kenny, author of 25 books (poetry and nonfiction), has been widely published in the United States and abroad. Her awards include first prize in the 2021 Allen Ginsberg Poetry Awards, New Jersey State Arts Council poetry fellowships, a Merton Poetry of the Sacred Award, and Kean University's Distinguished Alumni Award. Her book *A Lightness* . . . was a Paterson Poetry Prize finalist. She is poetry editor of *Tiferet* and founding director of the Carriage House Poetry Series. (p. 157)

Jane Kenyon (1947–1995) was an American poet and translator. While a student at the University of Michigan, Kenyon met the poet Donald Hall; though he was more than twenty years her senior, she married him in 1972, and they moved to Eagle Pond Farm, his ancestral home in New Hampshire. Kenyon was New Hampshire's poet laureate when she died in April 1995 from leukemia. When she died, she was working

on editing the now-classic *Otherwise: New and Selected Poems*, which was released posthumously in 1996. (p. 131)

Stuart Kestenbaum is the author of six collections of poems: *Pilgrimage* (Coyote Love Press) and *House of Thanksgiving, Prayers and Run-on Sentences, Only Now, How to Start Over*, and *Things Seemed to Be Breaking* (all from Deerbrook Editions). He has also written *The View from Here* (Brynmorgen Press), a book of brief essays on craft and community. He lives in Maine. (p. 123)

Michael Kleber-Diggs is the author of *Worldly Things*, which was awarded the 2020 Max Ritvo Poetry Prize. He was born and raised in Kansas and now lives in St. Paul, Minnesota. His work has appeared in Lit Hub, *The Rumpus, Rain Taxi*, McSweeney's Internet Tendency, *Water~Stone Review, Midway Review*, and *North Dakota Quarterly*. Michael teaches poetry and creative nonfiction through the Minnesota Prison Writers Workshop. (p. 17)

Thirteenth US Poet Laureate (2004–2006) **Ted Kooser** is a retired life insurance executive who lives on acreage near the village of Garland, Nebraska, with his wife, Kathleen Rutledge. His collection *Delights & Shadows* was awarded the Pulitzer Prize in Poetry in 2005. His poems have appeared in *The Atlantic*, *Hudson Review*, *Antioch Review*, *Kenyon Review*, and dozens of other literary journals. He is the author most recently of *Cotton Candy* (University of Nebraska Press) and *Marshmallow Clouds*, with Connie Wanek (Candlewick Press). (pp. 6, 116)

Jennifer G. Lai is a poet, visual artist, storyteller, and audio producer. Her work has appeared in *Pigeon Pages*, *ANOMALY*, *Canto Cutie*, *The Slowdown*, and *Angry Asian Man*, among others. Her visual work has participated in exhibitions at Jip Gallery and Olympia Gallery (A Place to Visit, V.3) and in Chelsea Market (Futures Ever Arriving). She currently lives in Brooklyn. Find her on Twitter @jenniferglai (p. 164)

Danusha Laméris is the author of two books: *The Moons of August* (Autumn House), which was chosen by Naomi Shihab Nye as the winner of the Autumn House Press Poetry Prize, and *Bonfire Opera* (University of Pittsburgh Press), which won the Northern California Book Award. Winner of the Lucille Clifton Legacy Award, she teaches in the Pacific University low-residency MFA program and co-leads with James Crews the global HearthFire Writing Community. She lives in Santa Cruz County, California. (pp. 49, 62, 121)

Alfred K. LaMotte has authored five books of poetry. A graduate of Yale University and Princeton Theological Seminary, LaMotte is a meditation teacher, interfaith college chaplain, and instructor in world religions. He lives in a small town on Puget Sound with his beloved wife, Anna, and loves to gather circles for meditation and poetry. (p. 125)

Dorianne Laux's sixth collection, *Only as the Day Is Long: New and Selected Poems*, was named a finalist for the 2020 Pulitzer Prize for Poetry. Her fifth collection, *The Book of Men*, was awarded the Paterson Prize, and her fourth book of poems, *Facts About the Moon*, won the Oregon Book Award. Laux is the coauthor of the celebrated *The Poet's Companion: A Guide to the Pleasures of Writing Poetry*. (p. 85)

Li-Young Lee was born in Djakarta, Indonesia, in 1957 to Chinese political exiles. He is the author of *The Undressing*; *Behind My Eyes*; *Book of My Nights*, which won the 2002 William Carlos Williams Award; *The City in Which I Love You*, which was the 1990 Lamont Poetry Selection; and *Rose*, which won the Delmore Schwartz Memorial Poetry Award. (p. 50)

Paula Gordon Lepp lives in South Charleston, West Virginia, with her husband and two almost-grown kids. She grew up in a rural community in the Mississippi Delta, and a childhood spent roaming woods and fields, climbing trees, and playing in the dirt instilled in her a love for nature that is reflected in her poems. Paula's work has been published in the anthologies *How to Love the World: Poems of Gratitude and Hope* and *The Mountain: An Anthology of Mountain Poems* (Middle Creek Publishing). (p. 7)

Annie Lighthart began writing poetry after her first visit to an Oregon old-growth forest and now teaches poetry wherever she can. Poems from her books *Iron String* and *Pax* have been featured on The Writer's Almanac and in many anthologies. Annie's work has been turned into music, used in healing projects, and has traveled farther than she has. She hopes you find a poem to love in this book, even if it is one she didn't write. (p. 140)

Ada Limón is the author of six poetry collections, including *The Hurting Kind* and *The Carrying*, which won the National Book Critics Circle Award. Her fourth book, *Bright Dead Things*, was named a finalist for the National Book Award, the Kingsley Tufts Poetry Award, and the National Book Critics Circle Award. A recipient of a Guggenheim Fellowship for Poetry, she was recently named US poet laureate. (pp. 53, 136)

Lois Lorimer is a Canadian poet, actor, and teacher. Her poems appear in the journals *Arc and Literary Review of Canada*, as well as many anthologies, including *The Bright Well* (Leaf Press) and *Heartwood* (League of Canadian Poets). Her first collection was *Stripmall Subversive* (Variety Crossing Press). A member of the League of Canadian Poets, Lois enjoys writing near water and believes in the power of poetry to heal and delight. (p. 158)

Alison Luterman's four books of poetry are *The Largest Possible Life*, *See How We Almost Fly*, *Desire Zoo*, and *In the Time of Great Fires*. Her poems and stories have appeared in *The Sun*, *Rattle*, *Salon*, *Prairie Schooner*, *Nimrod*, the *Atlanta Review*, *Tattoo Highway*, and elsewhere. She has written an ebook of personal essays, *Feral City*, half a dozen plays, a song cycle, as well as two

musicals, *The Chain* and *The Shyest Witch*. (p. 36)

Emilie Lygren is a poet and outdoor educator who holds a bachelor's degree in geology-biology from Brown University. Her poems have been published in *Thimble Literary Magazine*, *English Leadership Quarterly*, *Solo Novo*, and several other literary journals. Her first book of poems, *What We Were Born For* (Blue Light Press), won the Blue Light Book Award. She lives in San Rafael, California. (p. 97)

Marilyn McCabe's work has garnered her an Orlando Prize from A Room of Her Own Foundation; the Hilary Tham Capital Collection contest award from The Word Works, resulting in publication of her book of poems *Perpetual Motion*; and two artist grants from the New York State Council on the Arts. Her second book of poems, *Glass Factory*, was published in 2016. marilynonaroll.wordpress .com (p. 112)

Brooke McNamara is a poet, teacher, and ordained Zen monk and Dharma Holder. She has published two books of poems, *Bury the Seed* and *Feed Your Vow*, and is the recipient of the Charles B. Palmer Prize from the Academy of American Poets. Brooke has taught yoga studies at Naropa University and dance at University of Colorado–Boulder. She lives with her husband and two sons in Boulder. BrookeMcNamara.com (p. 65)

Rachel Michaud is a prize-winning poet and essayist. Her essays have been published in the *Washington Post* and *Hartford Courant* and broadcast on WAMC-Northeast Public Radio. Her poetry has appeared in literary journals and anthologies and been set to music. Michaud has worked on behalf of nonprofit organizations supporting food security, education, and the arts. She divides her time between Washington, DC, and Cambridge, New York. (p. 41)

Brad Aaron Modlin wrote *Everyone at This Party Has Two Names*, which won the Cowles Poetry Prize. *Surviving in Drought* (stories) won the Cupboard Pamphlet contest. His work has been the basis for orchestral scores, an art exhibition, an episode of *The Slowdown* with Ada Limón, and the premier episode of *Poetry Unbound* from On Being Studios. A professor and the Reynolds Endowed Chair of Creative Writing at University of Nebraska–Kearney, he teaches, coordinates the visiting writers' series, and gets chalk all over himself. (p. 153)

David Mook began writing poetry after the sudden death of his eight-year-old daughter, Sarah, a poet who began writing poems in kindergarten. *Each Leaf* (Freewheeling Press) includes poems written by Sarah. The Sarah Mook Poetry Contest honors the work of student poets in grades K–12. David lives in Vermont and teaches at Castleton University. (p. 160)

Marjorie Moorhead writes from the beautiful Connecticut River Valley at the Vermont–New Hampshire border. Having survived AIDS, Marjorie embraced poetry to tell her story and join in community with others. Her collection *Every Small Breeze* is forthcoming from Indolent Books. Marjorie's chapbooks are *Survival: Trees, Tides, Song* (FLP), and *Survival Part 2: Trees, Birds, Ocean, Bees* (Duck Lake Books). She is happy to have poems included in many anthologies and journals. (p. 128)

Tyler Mortensen-Hayes is a poet from Salt Lake City. His work has appeared in *Rattle*, *Frogpond*, and *Weber: The Contemporary West*. He holds an MFA from the University of New Mexico, where he was poetry editor of *Blue Mesa Review*. A student of Insight Meditation and Soto Zen, he hopes to become a teacher of meditation and mindfulness, using poetry as a quintessential practice. (p. 147)

Susan Musgrave lives on Haida Gwaii, islands in the North Pacific that lie equidistant from Luxor, Machu Picchu, Ninevah, and Timbuktu. The high point of her literary career was finding her name in the index of *Montreal's Irish Mafia*. She has published more than 30 books and has received awards in six categories: poetry, novels, nonfiction, food writing, editing, and books for children. Her new book of poetry is *Exculpatory Lilies*. (p. 78)

Mark Nepo has moved and inspired readers and seekers all over the world with his #1 *New York Times* bestseller *The Book of Awakening*. Beloved as a poet, teacher, and storyteller, Mark has been called "one of the finest spiritual guides of our time," "a consummate storyteller," and "an eloquent spiritual teacher." He has published 22 books and recorded 14 audio projects. Recent work includes *The Book of Soul* and *Drinking from the River of Light*, a Nautilus Award winner. marknepo.com and threeintentions.com (pp. 29, 42, 99, 103)

Robbi Nester explores the world from her desk in Southern California. She is the author of four books of poetry and editor of three anthologies. robbinester.net (p. 73)

Cristina M. R. Norcross is the editor of *Blue Heron Review*, the author of nine poetry collections, a multiple Pushcart Prize nominee, and an Eric Hoffer Book Award nominee. Her most recent collection is *The Sound of a Collective Pulse* (Kelsay Books). Cristina's work appears in *Lothlorien*, *Muddy River Poetry Review*, *Verse-Virtual*, the *Ekphrastic Review*, *Visual Verse*, and *Pirene's Fountain*, among others. She is the cofounder of Random Acts of Poetry & Art Day. cristinanorcross.com (p. 100)

Naomi Shihab Nye recently served as the Young People's Poet Laureate of the United States (Poetry Foundation). Her most recent books are *Everything Comes Next: Collected & New Poems*, *Cast Away (Poems about Trash)*, *The Tiny Journalist*, and *Voices in the Air—Poems for Listeners*. She also edited *Dear Vaccine: Global Voices*

Speak to the Pandemic with David Hassler and Tyler Meier. She lives in San Antonio, Texas. (p. 74)

January Gill O'Neil is an associate professor of English at Salem State University. She is the author of *Rewilding* (CavanKerry Press), a finalist for the 2019 Paterson Poetry Prize; *Misery Islands* (CavanKerry Press); and *Underlife* (CavanKerry Press). (pp. 26, 172)

Brad Peacock is a veteran and longtime organic farmer from Shaftsbury, Vermont, whose passion is to bring people closer to one another and the natural world. (p. 150)

Rosalie Sanara Petrouske's poem "Eating Corn Soup Under the Strawberry Moon" was one of six finalists in the 2020 Jack Grapes Poetry Prize from *Cultural Weekly*. Recently, she won First Place in the 2022 Poetry Box Chapbook Competition, for *Tracking the Fox*. An English professor at Lansing Community College in Lower Michigan, she has also been a finalist for the distinction of Upper Peninsula poet laureate. (p. 144)

Kathryn Petruccelli holds an MA in teaching English language learners and an obsession around the power of voice. Her work has appeared in places like the *Southern Review, Massachusetts Review, Hunger Mountain, Rattle, Tinderbox, SWWIM,* and *River Teeth's Beautiful Things.* She's been a Best of the Net nominee and a finalist for the Omnidawn Poetry Broadside Contest. Kathryn tour-guides at the Emily Dickinson Museum and teaches workshops for adults and teens.
poetroar.com (p. 132)

Andrea Potos is the author of *Her Joy Becomes* (Fernwood Press), *Marrow of Summer* and *Mothershell* (both from Kelsay Books), and *A Stone to Carry Home* (Salmon Poetry). Recent poems appear in *Poetry East, The Sun, Braided Way, Potomac Review,* and the anthologies *How to Love the World: Poems of Gratitude and Hope* and *The Path to Kindness: Poems of Connection and Joy.* (p. 11)

Rena Priest is a citizen of the Lhaq'temish (Lummi) Nation. Priest is the author of *Northwest Know-How: Beaches* (Sasquatch Books); *Sublime Subliminal* (Floating Bridge Press); and *Patriarchy Blues* (Moonpath Press), which received an American Book Award. Priest was appointed Washington State Poet Laureate in 2021 and is the 2022 Maxine Cushing Gray Distinguished Writing Fellow. She currently resides near her tribal community in Bellingham, Washington, where she was born and raised. (p. 143)

Alison Prine's debut collection of poems, *Steel* (Cider Press Review) was named a finalist for the 2017 Vermont Book Award. Her poems have appeared in *Ploughshares, Virginia Quarterly Review, Five Points, Harvard Review,* and *Prairie Schooner,* among others. She lives and works in Burlington, Vermont.
alisonprine.com (p. 34)

Laura Ann Reed's work has been anthologized in *How to Love the World: Poems of Gratitude and Hope,* and is forthcoming in the SMEOP anthology *HOT,* in addition to appearing in *Loch Raven, One Art, MacQueen's Quinterly,*

SWWIM, the *Ekphrastic Review*, *Willawaw*, and *Grey Sparrow Journal*, among other journals. Her chapbook *Shadows Thrown* is slated for publication by SunGold Editions. A San Francisco Bay Area native, Laura currently resides with her husband in western Washington. (p. 138)

Alberto Ríos was named Arizona's first poet laureate in 2013. He is the author of many poetry collections from Copper Canyon Press, including *Not Go Away Is My Name*; *A Small Story About the Sky*; *The Dangerous Shirt*; *The Theater of Night*; and *The Smallest Muscle in the Human Body*, which was nominated for a National Book Award. (p. 124)

Charles Rossiter, a National Endowment for the Arts fellowship recipient, hosts the biweekly podcast at poetryspokenhere.com. His poems are published in *Bennington Review*, *Paterson Literary Review*, *After Hours*, and more. Recent collections include *The Night We Danced with the Raelettes*, a memoir in poetry; *All Over America: Road Poems*; and *Green*

Mountain Meditations (all from FootHills Publishing). He has performed at the Nuyorican Poets Café, Green Mill, the Dodge Festival, Detroit Opera House, and Chicago Blues Festival. (p. 167)

Ellen Rowland creates, concocts, and forages when she's not writing. She is the author of *Light, Come Gather Me* and *Blue Seasons*, as well as the book *Everything I Thought I Knew*, essays on living, learning, and parenting. Her writing has appeared in *The Path to Kindness: Poems of Connection and Joy* and *Hope is a Group Project*. Her debut collection of full-length poems, *No Small Thing*, was published by Fernwood Press (2023). She lives off the grid with her family on an island in Greece. (pp. 8, 32)

Marjorie Saiser's seventh collection, *Learning to Swim* (Stephen F. Austin State University Press), contains both poetry and memoir. Her novel-in-poems, *Losing the Ring in the River* (University of New Mexico Press), won the WILLA Award for Poetry in 2014. Saiser's most recent book, *The Track the Whales Make: New & Selected Poems*, is available from University of Nebraska Press. poetmarge.com (p. 30)

Faith Shearin's books of poetry include *The Owl Question* (May Swenson Award); *Moving the Piano*; *Telling the Bees*; *Orpheus, Turning* (Dogfish Poetry Prize); *Darwin's Daughter*; and *Lost Language* (Press 53). She has received awards from Yaddo, the National Endowment for the Arts, and the Fine Arts Work Center in Provincetown. Her poems have been read on The Writer's Almanac and included in American Life in Poetry. She lives in Amherst, Massachusetts. (p. 90)

Derek Sheffield's collection *Not for Luck* was selected by Mark Doty for the 2019 Wheelbarrow Books Poetry Prize. His other books include *Through the Second Skin*, finalist for the Washington State Book Award; *Dear America*; and *Cascadia Field Guide: Art, Ecology, Poetry*. He is the poetry editor of Terrain.org. (p. 117)

Michael Simms's recent books include two collections of poetry, *American Ash* and *Nightjar* (both published by Ragged Sky Press), and a novel, *Bicycles of the Gods: A Divine Comedy* (published by Madville). Simms was the founding editor (1998–2016) of Autumn House Press and currently is the founding editor of *Vox Populi*, an online magazine of poetry, politics, and nature. He lives with his family in the historic neighborhood of Mount Washington overlooking Pittsburgh. (p. 127)

Maggie Smith is the author of the national bestsellers *Goldenrod* and *Keep Moving*, as well as *Good Bones*, *The Well Speaks of Its Own Poison*, and *Lamp of the Body*. Smith's poems and essays have appeared in The Best American Poetry, the *New York Times*, the *New Yorker*, the *Paris Review*, *Ploughshares*, and elsewhere. Smith's latest book is a memoir: *You Could Make This Place Beautiful*. (p. 23)

Holly Wren Spaulding is an interdisciplinary artist, teacher, and author of *Between Us*, *Familiars*, *If August*, and *Pilgrim* (all published by Alice Greene & Co). Spaulding's writing has appeared in *Michigan Quarterly Review*, *Witness*, *Poetry Northwest*, *The Ecologist*, and elsewhere. She is the founder and artistic director of Poetry Forge, where she offers workshops and an annual manuscript intensive. She lives in Maine. hollywrenspaulding.com (p. 51)

Nathan Spoon is an autistic poet with learning disabilities whose poems have appeared or are forthcoming in *American Poetry Review*, *Bennington Review*, *Gulf Coast*, Poem-a-Day, *Poetry*, *Poetry Daily*, and *swamp pink*. He is author of the debut collection *Doomsday Bunker* and the chapbook *Fail Better! Feel Great!!* He is editor of *Queerly* and an ally of timemedicine.org. (p. 139)

Kim Stafford directs the Northwest Writing Institute at Lewis & Clark College and is the author of a dozen books, including *The Muses Among Us: Eloquent Listening and Other Pleasures of the Writer's Craft* (University of Georgia Press) and *Singer Come from Afar* (Red Hen Press). He has taught writing in Scotland, Mexico, Italy, and Bhutan. He served as Oregon poet laureate (2018–2020). He teaches and travels to raise the human spirit. (pp. 94, 120)

Julie Cadwallader Staub writes from her home near Burlington, Vermont. Her poems have been published widely in literary and religious journals and anthologies, including *The Path to Kindness: Poems of Connection and Joy* and *Poetry of Presence*. Her poem "Milk" won the 2015 Ruth Stone Award, and the *Potomac Review* nominated "Turning" for a 2019 Pushcart Prize. She has two collections of poems: *Face to Face* (Cascadia Publishing) and *Wing Over Wing* (Paraclete Press). (p. 163)

Meghan Sterling (she/her) lives in Maine. Her work is forthcoming in the *Los Angeles Review*, *RHINO Poetry*, *Nelle*, *Poetry South*, and many others. *These Few Seeds* (Terrapin Books) was an Eric Hoffer Grand Prize finalist. *Self-Portrait with Ghosts of the Diaspora* (Harbor Editions), *Comfort the Mourners* (Everybody Press), and *View from a Borrowed Field* (Lily Poetry Review's Paul Nemser Book Prize) are all forthcoming in 2023. (p. 89)

Joshua Michael Stewart is the author of three poetry collections: *Break Every String, The Bastard Children of Dharma Bums*, and *Love Something*. His poems have appeared in the *Massachusetts Review, Salamander, Plainsongs, Brilliant Corners, South Dakota Review*, and many other publications. He lives in Ware, Massachusetts. joshuamichaelstewart.com (p. 68)

Jacqueline Suskin is the author of seven books, including *Every Day Is a Poem* (Sounds True) and *Help in the Dark Season* (Write Bloody). With her project Poem Store, Suskin has composed over 40,000 improvisational poems for patrons who chose a topic in exchange for a unique verse. She was honored by Michelle Obama as a Turnaround Artist, and her work has been featured in the *New York Times, Los Angeles Times, The Atlantic*, and other publications. jacquelinesuskin.com (pp. 70, 152)

Joyce Sutphen grew up on a small farm in Stearns County, Minnesota. Her first collection of poems, *Straight Out of View*, won the Barnard New Women Poets Prize; her recent books are *The Green House* (Salmon Poetry) and *Carrying Water to the Field: New and Selected Poems* (University of Nebraska Press). She is the Minnesota poet laureate and professor emerita of literature and creative writing at Gustavus Adolphus College. (p. 110)

Heather Swan's poems have appeared in such journals as *Terrain, The Hopper, Poet Lore, Phoebe*, and the *Raleigh Review*, and her book of poems, *A Kinship with Ash* (Terrapin Books), was published in 2020. Her nonfiction has appeared in *Aeon, Belt, Catapult, Emergence, ISLE*, and *Terrain*. Her book

Where Honeybees Thrive: Stories from the Field (Penn State Press) won the Sigurd F. Olson Nature Writing Award. She teaches environmental literature and writing at the University of Wisconsin–Madison. (p. 108)

Bradford Tice is the author of *Rare Earth* (New Rivers Press), which was named the winner of the 2011 Many Voices Project, and *What the Night Numbered* (Trio House Press), winner of the 2014 Trio Award. His poetry and fiction have appeared in such periodicals as *The Atlantic*, *North American Review*, the *American Scholar*, and *Epoch*, as well as in *The Best American Short Stories 2008*. (p. 161)

Angela Narciso Torres is the author of *Blood Orange*, winner of the Willow Books Literature Award for Poetry. Her recent collections include *To the Bone* (Sundress Publications) and *What Happens Is Neither* (Four Way Books). Her work has appeared in *Poetry*, *Missouri Review*, *Quarterly West*, *Cortland Review*, and *PANK*. Born in Brooklyn and raised in Manila, she serves as a senior and reviews editor for *RHINO Poetry*. (p. 44)

Rosemerry Wahtola Trommer lives on the banks of the San Miguel River in southwest Colorado. She co-hosts the Emerging Form podcast and Secret Agents of Change (a kindness cabal). Her poems have been featured on *A Prairie Home Companion*, American Life in Poetry, and *PBS Newshour*, as well as in *O, The Oprah Magazine*. Her collection *Hush* won the Halcyon Prize. She is also the author of *Naked for Tea* and *All the Honey* (Samara Press). Her one-word mantra: Adjust. (pp. 48, 166)

Susan Varon is a poet, artist, and Interfaith minister. She started writing in 1989 after her life was rearranged by a stroke. Her work has appeared in *Green Mountains Review*, *Notre Dame Review*, *Paterson Literary Review*, and the *Midwest Quarterly*, among many others. After living for 40 years in New York City, she moved to Taos, New Mexico, in April 2007, beckoned there by the Helene Wurlitzer Foundation artists' colony, the mountains, and the sky. (p. 69)

Connie Wanek was born in Wisconsin, raised in New Mexico, and lived for over a quarter century in Duluth. She is the author of *Bonfire* (New Rivers Press), winner of the New Voices Award; *Hartley Field* (Holy Cow! Press); and *On Speaking Terms* (Copper Canyon Press). In 2016, the University of Nebraska Press published Wanek's *Rival Gardens: New and Selected Poems* as part of Ted Kooser's Contemporary Poetry series. (p. 146)

Caroline Webster is a Vermont Artist Development Grant recipient, teacher, and Gateless writer. She has called many places home: Austria, North Carolina, Vermont, Korea, and Oman. The year 2020 brought her back to where she started, Virginia. In her work, she's grateful to support the Teachers in the Movement project and explore how educators' stories add to our understanding of history and influence today. She believes in the power of poetry to provide refuge and promote healing. (p. 102)

Laura Grace Weldon lives on a small ramshackle farm where she works as a book editor, teaches writing workshops, and maxes out her library card each week. Laura served as Ohio's 2019 Poet of the Year and is the author of four books, fifth on the way. lauragraceweldon.com (p. 142)

Diana Whitney writes across the genres in Vermont with a focus on feminism, mother-hood, and sexuality. Her work has appeared in the *New York Times*, the *San Francisco Chronicle*, the *Kenyon Review*, *Glamour*, *The Rumpus*, and many more. Diana's poetry debut, *Wanting It* (Harbor Mountain Press, 2014), won the Rubery Book Award, and her inclusive anthology, *You Don't Have to Be Everything: Poems for Girls Becoming Themselves* (Workman, 2021), became a YA bestseller and won the 2022 Claudia Lewis Award. diana-whitney.com (p. 13)

Michelle Wiegers is a poet, creative writer, and mind-body life coach based in southern Vermont. Her poems are inspired by her mind-body recovery from decades of chronic symptoms, the Vermont landscape, and her own backyard. Her work has appeared in *Birchsong*, *How to Love the World: Poems of Gratitude and Hope*, *The Path to Kindness: Poems of Connection and Joy*, and *Third Wednesday*, among others. In her coaching and teaching work, she is a passionate advocate for chronic pain and fatigue sufferers. michellewiegers.com (p. 66)

Katherine J. Williams, art therapist and clinical psychologist, was the director of the art therapy program at George Washington University, where she is now an associate professor emerita. Her poems have been published in journals and anthologies such as *Poet Lore*, the *Broadkill Review*, *3rd Wednesday*, *Delmarva Review*, *The Poet's Cookbook*, *The Widows' Handbook*, and *How to Love the World: Poems of Gratitude and Hope*. She is the author of *Still Life* (Cherry Grove). (p. 137)

Sarah Wolfson is the author of *A Common Name for Everything*, which won the A. M. Klein Prize for Poetry. Her poems have appeared in journals such as *AGNI*, *TriQuarterly*, *The Walrus*, *The Fiddlehead*, and *West Branch*. Her work has also been anthologized in *Rewilding: Poems for the Environment* and received notable mention in *Best Canadian Poetry*. Originally from Vermont, she now lives in Tiohtià:ke/Montreal, where she teaches writing at McGill University. (p. 77)

Lisa Zimmerman's poetry collections include *How the Garden Looks from Here* (Violet Reed Haas Poetry Award winner), *The Light at the Edge of Everything* (Anhinga Press), and *Sainted* (Main Street Rag). Her poetry and fiction have appeared in *Redbook*, *The Sun*, *SWWIM Every Day*, *Cave Wall*, and *Poet Lore*, among other journals. Her poems have been nominated for Best of the Net, five times for the Pushcart Prize, and included in *The Best Small Fictions 2020* anthology. (p. 106)

Yvonne Zipter is author of the poetry collections *The Wordless Lullaby of Crickets*, *Kissing the Long Face of the Greyhound*, *The Patience of Metal* (Lambda Literary Award finalist), and *Like Some Bookie God*; the Russian historical novel *Infraction*; and the nonfiction books *Diamonds Are a Dyke's Best Friend* and *Ransacking the Closet*. Her individual published poems are being sold in two repurposed toy-vending machines in Chicago, the proceeds of which support a local nonprofit organization. (p. 159)

CREDITS

"Archilochus Colubris" by José A. Alcántara, from *The Bitten World* (Tebot Bach, 2022). Reprinted with permission of author.

"What the Roses Said to Me" by Lahab Assef Al-Jundi, from *This Is It* (Kelsay Books, 2021). Reprinted by permission of author.

"Locust" by Julia Alvarez. Copyright © 2004 by Julia Alvarez. From *The Woman I Kept to Myself*, published by Algonquin Books of Chapel Hill. By permission of Susan Bergholz Literary Services, Lamy, NM. All rights reserved.

"First Snow" by James Armstrong, originally published in *Poetry East,* edited by Richard Jones.

"Hugging the Tree" by Zeina Azzam, from *Streetlight Magazine* (Issue no. 39, Fall 2021).

"Chestnut" by Rebecca Baggett from *The Woman Who Lives Without Money* (Regal House Publishing, 2022). Reprinted with permission of author.

"The Peace of Wild Things" by Wendell Berry from *New Collected Poems.* Copyright © 2012 by Wendell Berry. Reprinted with the permission of The Permissions Company, LLC on behalf of Counterpoint Press, counterpointpress.com.

"Swim Lessons" by George Bilgere, from *Blood Pages.* Copyright © 2018 Reprinted by permission of University of Pittsburgh Press.

"The Way We Love Something Small" Copyright © 2020 by Kimberly Blaeser. Originally published in Poem-a-Day on April 8, 2020 by the Academy of American Poets.

"Aubade" by Sally Bliumis-Dunn, originally published in *Beltway Poetry Quarterly.*

"Lately," by Laure-Anne Bosselaar, originally published in *Vox Populi.*

"Birdfoot's Grampa" by Joseph Bruchac, from *Entering Onondaga* (Cold Mountain Press, 1978). "Tutuwas" originally appeared in *Gwarlingo Sunday Poem.* Reprinted by permission of author.

"Ocean Love" by Carolyn Chilton Casas, originally published on grateful.org.

"Pocket" by Judith Chalmer, from *Minnow* (Kelsay Books, 2020). Reprinted by permission of author.

"Creed" by Patricia Clark, from *My Father on a Bicycle* (Michigan State University Press, 2005). Reprinted with permission of author.

"Essence" by Kai Coggin, from *Mining for Stardust* (Flower Song Press, 2021). Reprinted by permission of author.

"Encounter" by Sharon Corcoran, from *The Two Worlds* (Middle Creek Publishing & Audio, 2021). Reprinted by permission of author.

"Tomatoes" by James Crews, originally published in *Vox Populi.*

"This Summer Day" by Barbara Crooker, from *A Small Rain* (Purple Flag, 2014). Reprinted by permission of author.

"Cherry Blossoms" by Toi Derricotte, from *The Undertaker's Daughter* Copyright © 2011. Reprinted by permission of University of Pittsburgh Press.

the permission of The Permissions Company, LLC on behalf of Graywolf Press, graywolfpress.org.

"Home in the Woods" by Linda Hogan, from *Dark. Sweet.: New & Selected Poems*. Copyright © 2014 by Linda Hogan. Reprinted with the permission of The Permissions Company, LLC on behalf of Coffee House Press, coffeehousepress.org.

"The Honeybee" by Jacqueline Jules, originally published in *ONE ART*, edited by Mark Danowsky.

"Survivor" by Adele Kenny from *What Matters* (Welcome Rain Publishers, 2011). Reprinted with permission of author.

"In Several Colors" by Jane Kenyon, from *Collected Poems*. Copyright © 2005 by The Estate of Jane Kenyon. Reprinted with the permission of The Permissions Company, LLC on behalf of Graywolf Press, graywolfpress.org.

"Holding the Light" by Stuart Kestenbaum, from *Only Now* (Deerbrook Editions, 2013). Copyright © 2013 by Stuart Kestenbaum. Used by permission of author.

"The Grove" by Michael Kleber-Diggs, from *Worldly Things*. Copyright © 2021 by Michael Kleber-Diggs. Reprinted with the permission of The Permissions Company, LLC on behalf of Milkweed Editions, milkweed.org.

"In Early April" by Ted Kooser, reprinted by permission of author. "A Glint," from *A Man with a Rake* (Pulley Press, 2022). Reprinted by permission of author and publisher.

"In My Mind's Coral, Mother Still Calls Us from Inside" by Jennifer G. Lai originally appeared in *Pigeon Pages*.

"Nothing Wants to Suffer" by Danusha Laméris, reprinted by permission of author. "Dust" by Danusha Laméris, from *Bonfire Opera*. Copyright © 2020. Reprinted by permission of University of Pittsburgh Press.

"Gentle" by Alfred K. LaMotte, from *Savor Eternity One Moment at a Time* (St. Julian Press, 2016). Reprinted by permission of the author.

"My Mother's Colander" by Dorianne Laux, from *Only As the Day Is Long: New and Selected Poems*. Copyright © 2019. Used by permission of W. W. Norton & Company, Inc.

"To Hold" by Li-Young Lee, from *Behind My Eyes*. Copyright © 2008 by Li-Young Lee. Used by permission of W. W. Norton & Company, Inc.

"Let This Day" by Annie Lighthart, from *Pax* (Fernwood Press, 2021). Reprinted by permission of the author.

"Joint Custody" and "It's the Season I Often Mistake" by Ada Limón, from *The Hurting Kind*. Copyright © 2022 by Ada Limón. Reprinted with the permission of The Permissions Company, LLC on behalf of Milkweed Editions, milkweed.org.

"Rescue Dog" by Lois Lorimer, from *Stripmall Subversive* (Variety Crossing Press, 2012) and the anthology *The Bright Well* (Leaf Press, 2012). Reprinted by permission of author.

"Heavenly Bodies" by Alison Luterman, from *In the Time of Great Fires* (Catamaran Press, 2020). Reprinted by permission of author.

"Meditation" by Emilie Lygren, from *What We Were Born For* (Blue Light Press, 2021). Reprinted by permission of author.

"Web" by Marilyn McCabe, originally published in *Stone Canoe.*

"One Candle Now, Then Seven More" by Brad Aaron Modlin originally appeared in *Tupelo Quarterly.*

"Tomatoes on the Windowsill After Rain" by Susan Musgrave, from *When the World Is Not Our Home: Selected Poems 1985-2000* (Thistledown, 2009). Reprinted by permission of author.

"Under the Temple," "Stopped Again by the Sea," "Art Lesson," and "The Clearing" by Mark Nepo, from *The Half-Life of Angels* (Freefall Books, 2023). Reprinted by permission of author.

"Rot" by Robbi Nester originally appeared in *Verse-Virtual.*

"Breathing Peace" by Cristina M. R. Norcross, from *The Sound of a Collective Pulse* (Kelsay Books, 2021).

"Little Farmer" by Naomi Shihab Nye. Reprinted by permission of author.

"For Ella" by January Gill O'Neil reprinted by permission of author.

"How to Love" by January Gill O'Neil, from *Rewilding.* Copyright © 2018 by January Gill O'Neil. Reprinted with the permission of The Permissions Company, LLC on behalf of CavanKerry Press, Ltd., cavankerry.org.

"True North" by Rosalie Sanara Petrouske originally appeared in *Tracking the Fox* (The Poetry Box Chapbook Prize, 2022).

"Crocheting in December" by Andrea Potos, from *Her Joy Becomes* (Fernwood Press, 2023). Reprinted with permission of author.

"Tour of a Salmonberry" by Rena Priest, originally published in *A Dozen Nothing* (2021). Reprinted with per-mission of the author.

"The Broken" by Alberto Ríos, from *A Small Story About the Sky.* Copyright © 2015 by Alberto Ríos. Reprinted with the permission of The Permissions Company, LLC on behalf of Copper Canyon Press, coppercanyonpress.org.

"What Branches Hold" and "The Way the Sky Might Taste" by Ellen Rowland, from *No Small Thing* (Fernwood Press, 2023). Reprinted by permission of author.

"Crane Migration, Platte River" by Marjorie Saiser, from *The Woman in the Moon* (University of Nebraska Press, Backwaters Series, 2018). Reprinted by permission of author.

"My Daughter Describes the Tarantula" by Faith Shearin, from *Telling the Bees* (SFA University Press, 2015). Reprinted by permission of author.

"For Those Who Would See" by Derek Sheffield, from *Not for Luck* (Wheelbarrow Books, 2021). Reprinted by permission of author.

"Sometimes I Wake Early" by Michael Simms, from *Nightjar* (Ragged Sky Press, 2021).

"First Fall" by Maggie Smith, from *Good Bones: Poems.* Copyright © 2017 by Maggie Smith. Reprinted with the permission of The Permissions Company, LLC on behalf of Tupelo Press, tupelopress.org.

"Primitive Objects" by Holly Wren Spaulding, from *Pilgrim* (Alice Greene & Co., 2014). Reprinted with permission of author.

"Poem of Thankfulness" by Nathan Spoon originally published in *Blood Orange Review.*

"Wren's Nest in a Shed near Aurora" and "Advice from a Raindrop" by Kim Stafford, from *Singer Come from Afar.* Copyright © 2021 by

ACKNOWLEDGMENTS

Boundless gratitude once again to the staff at Storey Publishing for believing in these necessary collections of poetry, especially Deborah Balmuth, Liz Bevilacqua, Alee Moncy, Melinda Slaving, Jennifer Travis, Hannah Fries, and everyone else who supported this book. I'm grateful for the community of poets who contributed so generously to this anthology, which would not exist without them. Thanks especially to the following poets for their ongoing inspiration: Ted Kooser, Naomi Shihab Nye, Rosemerry Wahtola Trommer, Jane Hirshfield, Danusha Laméris, Michael Simms, Mark Nepo, Michelle Wiegers, Jacqueline Suskin, Kim Stafford, and Mark Danowsky. One of the greatest gifts of this past year was getting to know the poetry and heart of Nikita Gill, whose beautiful Foreword is a poem in and of itself. I appreciate the ongoing support of my Peacock and Crews families, who finally see what all those years of reading and writing have led to. I also want to thank the readers who have written to me about the lifesaving power of these anthologies, and who use them in hospitals, churches, classrooms, therapy sessions, wellness retreats, and yoga centers: I hold your notes close to my heart, and please don't ever hesitate to reach out. As always, I thank my husband, Brad Peacock, for keeping my wonder for this world alive and well each day.